BRITISH
InteriorDesign

The Deutsche Nationalbibliothek lists this publication in the Deutsche Nationalbibliografie; detailed bibliographical data are available on the internet at http://dnb.d-nb.de.

ISBN 978-3-03768-054-4
© 2010 by Braun Publishing AG
www.braun-publishing.ch

1st edition 2010

Project coordinator and English editing texts: Judith Vonberg
Translation: Chris van Uffelen (German version)
Graphic concept: Michaela Prinz, Berlin

BRITISH
InteriorDesign

Michelle Galindo

Content | Inhalt

Preface Great Britain has a long tradition of design dating back to the 18th century with the beginnings of the Industrial Revolution. Since then, the largest island state in Europe has produced designers who have gone on to earn recognition worldwide, among them industrial and furniture designers such as Jasper Morrison and Barber Osgerby. Practitioners of British interior design often work within two disciplines, the historicist world of interiors genre and the rational school in which they are taught; they work within a framework that interacts both with tradition and with the client's particular taste. The world of interiors is a field which reflects the cultural evolution of the spaces we inhabit.

British Interior Design offers a glimpse into a wide range of interiors from private homes to museums, representing the wonderful eccentricity associated with British design through a wild array of styles from classical to kitsch interiors, from old spaces modernised and manipulated to entirely new interiors. This book crosses the threshold to reveal an evocative and inspiring combination of the traditional and the modern - from floral and romantic to bold, colourful and quirky British interiors juxtaposed with soft coloured textiles and walls of modern art. It features the work of well-known and established British interior designers, such as Jonathan Tuckey, who inserts new

Großbritannien hat eine lange Design-Tradition, die bis in das 18. Jahrhundert, zu den Anfängen der industriellen Revolution, zurückreicht. Seit dieser Zeit hat der größte Inselstaat in Europa Designer hervorgebracht, die weltweit Anerkennung erlangen, unter ihnen Industriedesigner und Möbel-Designer wie Jasper Morrison und Barber Osgerby. Britische Innenarchitekten bewegen sich oft zwischen zwei Disziplinen, zwischen der historisch geprägten Welt der Innenraumgestaltung auf der einen Seite und der rationalen Schule, die sie gelehrt wurden, andererseits. Sie arbeiten innerhalb eines Rahmens, auf den sowohl Tradition als auch der individuelle Geschmack des Klienten aufeinander treffen. Die Welt der Innenraumgestaltung ist ein Feld, das die kulturelle Entwicklung der Räume widerspiegelt, die wir bewohnen.

British Interior Design bietet einen Einblick in eine Reihe von Innenräumen, von privaten Häusern bis zu Museen, die die wunderbare Exzentrik britischen Designs mit einer Reihe von Stilen, von klassisch bis Kitsch vorstellen, ebenso wie Umbauten von Bestehendem zu völlig neuen Welten. Dieses Buch präsentiert anregende Kombinationen aus Tradition und Moderne, floralen romantischen und gewagten, farbig verzierten britischen Innenräumen, kombiniert mit weichen farbigen Textilien und moderner Kunst an den Wänden. Es zeigt Arbeiten wie die des wohlbe-

forms into existing structures and mixes old and new to make defiantly contemporary interiors and Kit Kemp, who fuses contemporary design elements with a solid, classical setting and draws extensively on British interiors and art. The interiors of Rabih Hage go beyond the superpolished to the natural and rough, creating contrasts with luxurious soft furnishings and burnished objects.

The interiors presented in this book bridge the gap between the classic and the modern with iconic styles and design classics from the 1920s to the modern day, featuring furniture such as the Love Seat designed by Ercol in 1954 using the steam-bent wood technique and Tom Dixon's iconic Mirror Ball Light, which features prominently in several of the projects. Some interiors steal back the 1980s English country house style, epitomised by bold, floral fabrics, painted furniture, displays of brightly patterned china, and co-ordinated ruffles and swags. Others make use of David Hicks' signature 1960s style of bright colours and strong patterns. Each one of the interiors reflects both a deeply entrenched sense of history and familiar, to the point of predictable, iconography that place British interior design at the forefront of global design, embracing international styles and influences as much as its own.

kannten britischen Innenarchitekten Jonathan Tuckey, der neue Formen in bestehende Strukturen einsetzt und der durch einen gekonnten Mix von Alt und Neu umwerfend moderne Innenräume schafft. Oder die von Kit Kemp, die zeitgenössische Designelemente mit einer soliden, klassischen Einrichtung verschmelzen lässt und diese mit britischer Kunst kombiniert. Das Design von Rabih Hage hat nichts mit hochglänzenden Einrichtungen zu tun, sondern ist natürlich und rauh, er schafft Kontraste mit luxuriösen weichen Einrichtungen und polierten Objekten.

Die in diesem Buch präsentierten Innenräume schließen die Lücke zwischen Klassik und Moderne, mit kultigen Objekten und Designklassikern von den 1920er Jahren bis heute. Möbel wie der Love Seat, 1954 von Ercol mit ganz neuen Techniken entworfen, und die heutzutage kultige, hochglänzende Kugelleuchte von Tom Dixon, welche in einer Vielzahl von Projekten eingesetzt wird, werden auch heute noch gerne verwendet. Einige Projekte greifen den englischen Landhaus-Stil der 1980er Jahre auf, der durch bedruckte Blumenstoffe und bemalte Möbel verkörpert wird. Andere zitieren den 1960er Jahre-Stil von David Hick mit hellen Farben und starken Mustern.

Jedes der Projekte spiegelt ein tiefes Verständnis für Geschichte wider, das die britische Innenarchitektur in die erste Reihe weltweiten Designs stellt, auch weil es internationale Stile und Einflüsse so sehr aufnimmt wie seine eigenen.

office

Typical of British interior design is...

injecting a sense of humour and allowing the people to personalise a space and make it their own.

Wieden+Kennedy's London Headquarters

Featherstone Young

Address: T Block, The Old Truman Brewery, 91 Brick Lane, London E1 6QL. **Client:** Wieden+Kennedy. **Completion:** 2009, original: 1950. **Main function:** Office. **Materials:** Timber & steel structure. **Main finishes:** Glass, steel, concrete and rubber.

The interior treatment for this new office space was not only to provide the progressive agency with dynamic workspace for their staff but also create a multi-functional event space to encourage collaborations with creative partners and their clients. One floor is dominated by a large flexible auditorium space that can host a range of events from one-to-one meetings to large-scale music performances for up to 160 people. Bespoke retractable lights enable the change of atmosphere and wire-framed construction work lights in cluster arrangements emulate a chandelier effect. Off this main space are a series of garage lock-ups that can function either as hideaway spaces for private activities or extensions of the main space. All the spaces were designed to be fun and flexible. Design elements such as the 'stairway to heaven' and the red-tunnelled corridor ('a mouth with its tongue sticking out') inject a sense of humour. Simple, everyday materials and the use of bright colours such as yellow, red and green complement the industrial aesthetic of the 1950s building.

Der Ausbau dieses neuen Firmensitzes diente nicht nur dazu, neue Arbeitsplätze zu schaffen. Als Hauptsitz sollen die Räume auch repräsentativen Charakter haben und als Multifunktions-Fläche dienen, um die Zusammenarbeit mit anderen kreativen Partnern und Kunden zu befruchten. Auf einer Etage findet man zum Beispiel einen Saal, in dem verschiedene Veranstaltungen stattfinden können, vom kleinen Meeting bis zu großen Konzerten, bei dem bis zu 160 Menschen Platz finden. Licht spielte bei dem Umbau eine große Rolle: die Licht-Stimmung kann gesteuert werden und durch die in Trauben aufgehängten Baustellen-Leuchten entsteht eine kronleuchterartige Wirkung. Abseits des Hauptraumes findet man eine Reihe von kleineren Räumen, die entweder als Rückzugs-Räume fungieren können oder den Hauptraum erweitern können. Alle Räume wurden flexibel gestaltet. Designelemente wie die „Stairway to Heaven" und der rote Tunnel-Flur („ein Mund mit seiner ausgestreckten Zunge") zeigen deutlichen Sinn für Humor. Einfache Materialien und der Gebrauch von starken Farben wie gelb, rot und grün ergänzen die industrielle Ästhetik des 50er Jahre-Baus.

← Internal view of red tunnel. Innenansicht des roten Tunnels.

← ← Entrance area and stair tongue. Eingangsbereich mit Treppenaufgang.
← Bathroom graffiti. Badezimmer-Graffiti.
↑ Floor plans. Grundrisse.
↙ Stairway to heaven. „Stairway to Heaven".
↓ Garage lock-ups. Rückzugsräume.

CAN YOU
PLAY NICELY
WITH OTHER
CREATIVE
MINDS?

PLATFORM.WK.COM

Typical of British interior design is...
creating a playful yet practical solution.

72 Rivington Street

The Klassnik Corporation

Address: 72 Rivington Street, London EC2A 3AY. **Client:** YCN. **Completion:** 2009. **Main function:** Office, studios, gallery and shop. **Materials:** Plywood (polypropylene/birch faced and shuttering), polished concrete, perspex mirror, Egan Versa whiteboard sheet, Bisley steel cabinets.

72 Rivington Street, Shoreditch, houses design agency YCN. It includes a gallery area, library, shop, office, studios and roof terrace. The ground floor gallery is defined by irregularly shaped mobile objects; a playful kit of parts including plinths, vitrines, shelves, and steps configurable to the changing requirements of whatever is happening that day. The objects fit together like a three-dimensional jigsaw. Black chalkboard surfaces serve as special announcements canvases, playfully providing a solution to a practical problem. A concealed mirrored door leads upstairs where an elegant polypropylene coated plywood ribbon forms desk surfaces at a variety of levels, folding to create threshold archways within the space. Ready-made steel drawer units penetrate the shuttering ply plinth for storage and staggered plywood boxes with various widths of whiteboard door visually disintegrate the surface of the walls whilst also acting as an adaptable labelling system. A fun and flexible creative work environment.

Das Design-Büro YCN befindet sich in der 72 Rivington Street in Shoreditch. Zum Haus gehören eine Galerie, eine Bibliothek, ein Laden, Büroflächen und eine Dach-Terrasse. Die Galerie im Erdgeschoss wird durch unregelmäßig geformte und bewegliche Gegenstände definiert; eine spielerische Einrichtung aus Vitrinen, Regalen und Treppen, die sich jeden Tag den geänderten Anforderungen anpassen. Die Möbel passen zusammen wie ein dreidimensionales Puzzle. Ihre Oberflächen fungieren als Tafel und können beschrieben werden. Eine verborgene Spiegeltür führt ins Obergeschoss, wo ein elegantes, mit Polypropylen beschichtetes Band aus Sperrholz Oberflächen in verschiedenen Höhen formt, die zu Schreibtischen werden. Es faltet sich weiter durch den Raum und kreiert Torbögen innerhalb des Raumes, die verschiedene Zonen markieren. Regalböden aus Sperrholz mit verschieden breiten, verschiebbaren, Whiteboard-Paneelen, lösen visuell die Oberfläche der Wände auf, und dienen als flexibles und spielerisches Beschriftungs-System.

← First floor: plywood ribbon of desks. Band aus Sperrholz formt die Schreibtische.

↖ Kit of mobile furniture elements. Bewegliche Möbel-Elemente.
↑ Desk ribbon archways create thresholds. Band aus Sperrholz formt auch Durchgänge.
← Playful sculptural display objects. Spielerischer und skulptural wirkender Stauraum.
↗ Library room divider object. Raumteiler als Objekt und Bibliothek.
↘ Ground floor section and floor plan. Schnitt durch das Erdgeschoss und Grundriss.
↘↘ Meeting table extends through window. Der Besprechungstisch erstreckt sich durch das Fenster.

GROUND FLOOR SECTION BB

LENDING LIBRARY....SPECIAL OFFERS..GET THEM NOW!!

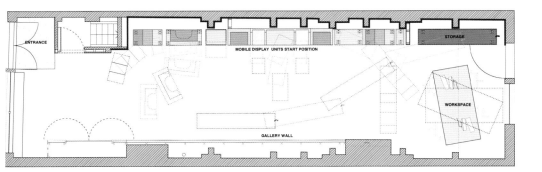

ENTRANCE

MOBILE DISPLAY UNITS START POSITION

STORAGE

WORKSPACE

GALLERY WALL

Typical of British interior design is...

rich in detail and a sense of the unexpected.

Manchester Square

SHH

Address: 10 Manchester Square, London W1U 3NL. **Artist:** Hugo Dalton. **Completion:** 2008. **Main function:** Office. **Original materials:** Marble mosaic floor tiles, marble-inlaid fireplaces and highly detailed ceiling cornicing. **New materials:** Black-stained white french oak, woven vinyl floortile, black herringbone timber and dark grey velvet drapes.

SHH was asked to create a 'high impact, 21st century office interior with a strong personality' with more in common with a gentlemen's club than a traditional office space. Although the property was made up of a classic (and Grade II listed) Georgian townhouse, the client was very open to a sense of contrast for the scheme, favouring a highly contemporary treatment. The generous per capita space was exploited with very individual rooms with differing personalities, achieved with varied colour saturation and differing degrees of formality. Bespoke lighting and art underline the individuality of this project, including two statement contemporary chandeliers, made to order and designed by Michael Anastassiades and four wall projections by artist Hugo Dalton. The artist produced a series of sketches of ballet dancers morphed with floral motifs, which were then laser-cut onto stainless steel discs and fitted into ceiling-mounted projectors.

Der Auftrag verlangte „eine Bürogestaltung mit hoher Effizienz und ausdrucksstarkem Charakter für das 21. Jahrhundert" zu schaffen. Sie sollte eher einem Gentlemen's Club als herkömmlichen Büroräumen ähneln. Der denkmalgeschützte Bestand eines georgianischen Stadthauses wurde entsprechend dem Wunsch des Auftraggebers nach einer modernen Formfindung und seinem Interesse an kontrastierenden Elementen neu ausgestattet. Die großzügige pro Kopf-Fläche wurde für sehr individuelle Räumlichkeiten genutzt. Unterschiedliche Farbsättigungen und Grade an Seriosität bewerkstelligen dies. Besondere Lampenmodelle und Kunstwerke unterstreichen die Individualität, darunter auch zwei speziell angefertigte zeitgenössische Kronleuchter von Michael Anastassiades, sowie vier Wandprojektionen des Künstlers Hugo Dalton. Der Künstler fertigte eine Skizzenreihe von Ballett-Tänzern an und verwandelte sie in florale Motive, die dann mittels Laser in Edelstahl geschnittenen und in deckenintegrierte Projektionsvorrichtungen eingebracht wurden.

← First Floor Executive Office. Geschäftsleitungszimmer, erstes Obergeschoss.

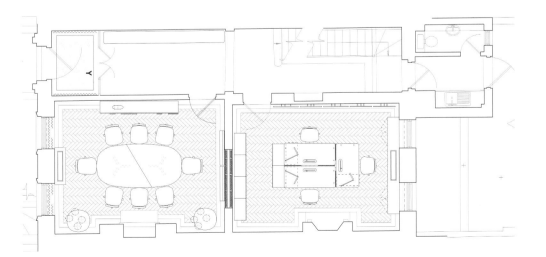

hotel,

bar, restaurant

Typical of British interior design is...

designing with layers and enhancing the past with contemporary design.

Rough Luxe Hotel

Rabih Hage

Address: 1 Birkenhead Street, London WC1H8BA. **Client:** Rough Luxe Hotel Ltd. **Completion:** 2008. **Main function:** Hotel.
Materials: Exposed floorboards, partially sanded walls, and bespoke furniture and day beds designed by Rabih Hage.

Rough Luxe is the antithesis to conventional hotels with air-conditioned constancy, marbled flooring, polished finishes and bland colours. It is a fascinating blend of urban archaeology, partially sanded surfaces, bare floorboards, chipped paint and rough edges mingled with gloriously opulent contemporary wallpaper and modern art plus top quality furnishings. Early on in the refurbishment, layers of wallpaper were peeled away to reveal decoration ideas from centuries ago. This intriguing 'archaeology' of interior design was kept and remains tangible in every room of this narrow town house. Breakfast is served in the basement dining room next door to the original 1960s utilitarian kitchen; guests sit around a table made of wood salvaged from Brighton Pier beneath an imposing ceiling photo of a Renaissance dome. The nine intimate and comfortable rooms with their original light fittings and door fixtures beguile with their period charm and obvious wear and tear.

Rough Luxe ist die Antithese zu den herkömmlichen Hotels mit konstanter Klimatisierung, Marmorfußböden, polierten Oberflächen und faden Farben. Es ist eine faszinierende Mischung aus städtischer Archäologie, teilweise handgeschliffenen Oberflächen, nackten Dielen, abgesplittertem Lack, Ecken und Kanten, vermischt mit herrlich opulenten zeitgenössischen Tapeten, moderner Kunst und hochwertigen Möbeln. Schon früh in der Sanierung wurden Tapetenschichten entfernt, um die Dekoration vergangener Jahrhunderte freizulegen. Diese faszinierende Archäologie des Interieurs wurde erhalten und bleibt in jedem Zimmer des schmalen Stadthauses erfahrbar. Das Frühstück wird im Esszimmer im Keller neben der ursprünglich aus den 1960er Jahren stammenden Küche serviert. Die Gäste sitzen an einem Tisch aus Holz, der vom Brightoner Pier geborgen wurde, unterhalb eines imposanten Fotos einer Renaissance-Kuppel. Die neun intimen und komfortablen Zimmer mit ihren originalen Lampen und Türbeschlägen betören mit historischem Charme und offensichtlicher Abnutzung.

← A portrait of Gilbert and George hangs in the lobby. Ein Doppelporträt von Gilbert and George in der Lobby.

←← En-suite bathrooms complete with burnished copper bathtubs.
Bäder der Hotelzimmer mit polierten kupfernen Badewannen.
← Bathroom clean and luxurious but designed to look a bit rough around
the edges. Sauberes und luxuriöses Badezimmer, rustikal und kantig
gestaltet.
↙ A print of a lavish opulent interior serves as a great contrast to
the unplastered walls. Die Grafik eines großzügigen und opulenten
Innenraums kontrastiert mit der unverputzten Wand.
↓ Coffee bar. Café.

Typical of British interior design is...
the carefully selected palette of
contemporary colours and materials.

Landau Restaurant

David Collins

Address: Portland Place, London W1B 1JA. **Client:** Langham Hotels. **Completion:** 2008. **Main function:** Restaurant. **Materials:** Brushed gilded timber wall panelling, custom-designed dining chairs upholstered in embossed leathers in a palette of pale gold, jade green and pastel blue.

Guests enter through an atmospherically lit hallway connecting the entrance lobby to the dining room. This vaulted passageway, theatrically displaying the restaurant's extensive wine collection, is paved in limestone and lined with exquisite glass-fronted wine cabinets. The existing restaurant has been transformed into a graceful lozenge-shape by dramatic restructuring of the internal architecture. Brushed gilded timber wall panelling and a trio of bespoke antique brass chandeliers, bearing lanterns inspired by Chinese bells, complement the inherent grandeur of the room. Subtle, mid-level lighting imbues the space with a shimmery, golden light. Custom-designed dining chairs upholstered in embossed leathers in a palette of pale gold, jade green and pastel blue lend a fresh, contemporary feel. Two booths, each accommodating six people, are housed within circular snugs recessed off the main room, with screens providing the luxury of private dining.

Gäste betreten das Restaurant durch einen atmosphärisch beleuchteten Flur, der die Eingangshalle mit dem Speisesaal verbindet. Dieser mit Kalkstein verkleidete Gewölbegang inszeniert die umfassende Wein-Sammlung des Restaurants, der Weg ist von gläsernen und hinterleuchteten Weinregalen gesäumt. Das ursprüngliche Restaurant wurde durch drastisches Umstrukturieren des Innenraumes in einen ovalen Raum umgewandelt. Die gebürstete vergoldete Wandverkleidung und drei maßangefertigte, antike Messing-Kronleuchter, ergänzen die natürliche Pracht des Raumes. Das raffinierte Lichtkonzept taucht den Raum in goldenes Licht. Maßgeferigte Stühle, mit geprägtem Leder in gold, jadegrün und lavendel verleihen dem Raum ein frisches und modernes Gesicht. Zwei Nischen, die jeweils Platz für sechs Personen bieten, befinden sich abseits des Hauptraumes in einem runden Erker. Sie können mit Schiebetüren geschlossen werden und bieten so den Luxus eines Privatdinners.

← Booths housed within circular snugs. Das Separee im runden Erker.

↖ Chairs upholstered in embossed leathers. Gepolsterte, mit geprägtem Leder bezogene Stühle.

↑ Dining room. Blick in den Speisesaal.

← Vaulted passageway paved in limestone and lined with exquisite glass-fronted wine cabinets. Im Gewölbegang aus Kalkstein werden die Weinregale durch eine Glasfront zur Vitrine.

↗ Interior view into banquette seating. Ansicht in den Bankettraum.

↘ Floor plan. Grundriss.

↘↘ Brushed gilded timber wall panelling. Die Wandverkleidung wurde vergoldet und gebürstet.

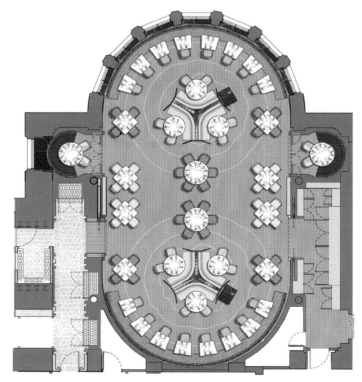

Typical of British interior design is...

taking reference of the architectural setting in the interior.

Paramount Bar

Tom Dixon, Design Research Studio

Address: Centre Point, 101-103 New Oxford Street, London WC1A 1DD. **Client:** Pierre Condou (Executive Director), Paramount and Century clubs. **Completion:** 2008. **Main function:** Private members club, restaurant and bar. **Materials:** Reclaimed timber flooring, timber joinery, metal wall panels, metal bars, metal screens, Tom Dixon furniture and lighting.

Paramount is the latest of London's exclusive members' clubs. Design Research Studio was invited to create something very special, to differentiate the club from stiff competition. The design concept is inspired by the architecture of the building, a Brutalist aesthetic in geometric forms. Shapes found in the concrete of the building façade are reintroduced to the interior through the design of custom items such as bars, wall panelling and furniture. Hard-edged materials such as concrete and stone were widely used to create a blend of 1960s retro and futurism. Located on levels 31, 32 and 33 of this landmark building, the design ensures that the spectacular view remains the key asset for the club. This is done by directing all internal light away from the windows and using matt finishes wherever possible.

Paramount ist der jüngste der exklusiven Mitglieder-Clubs Londons. Design Research Studio wurde geladen, ein außergewöhnliches Ambiente zu schaffen, das den Club von den Mitbewerbern abhebt. Das Entwurfskonzept wurde durch die Architektur des Gebäudes inspiriert, einem Bau in den geometrischen Formen des Brutalismus. Die Betonformen der Fassade wurden im Inneren durch die Gestaltung eigenständiger Elemente wie Bars, Wandverkleidungen und Möbeln aufgegriffen. Hartkantige Materialien wie Beton und Stein wurden genutzt um einen 1960er Jahre Retro-Futurismus zu schaffen. Das Design gewährleistet zugleich, dass die spektakuläre Aussicht aus dem 31. bis 33. Stockwerk des denkmalgeschützten Gebäudes der wichtigste Aktivposten des Clubs bleibt. Die Lichtführung von den Fenstern weg in den Raum und die nach Möglichkeit immer matten Oberflächenmaterialien tragen hierzu bei.

← The Red Room with spectacular panoramic city view. Der rote Raum mit spektakulärer Aussicht auf Lichter und Landschaft der Stadt.

↖ Bar. Bar.
↑ Bathroom. Toiletten.
← Interior of The Red Room. Interieur des roten Raums.
↗ Lounge. Lounge.
↘ Copper bar island. Kupferne Barinsel.
↘↘ Lounge with city views. Lounge mit Stadtansicht.

Typical of British interior design is...

building the future in a
space from the past.

Home House

Zaha Hadid Architects

Address: 20 Portman Square, London W1H 6LW. **Design collaborator:** Patrik Schumacher. **Original building architect:** James Wyatt. **Completion:** 2008. **Main function:** Bar. **Materials:** Fibre glass, resin, fabric and lacquered finish.

Zaha Hadid Architects' first London interior for two decades explodes within the Georgian restoration of the ground floor at Home House. The furniture installations, in saturated Georgian colours, flow through the bar, entrance, and reception rooms to create an interior landscape of sculptural islands. The sinuous forms follow the fluid geometries of natural systems and distortions. James Wyatt's original programmed spaces are recalled in the functionality of the composition's fluid and fresh forms. The islands float between history and future, inviting a dialogue between past and present, elasticity and solidity and craftsmanship spanning three centuries. The bar environment is dominated by the bar itself, a structure occupied by the members and guests who become part of the experience. A greater degree of warmness and intimacy was achieved in the lounge, which was developed as a horizontal field of disparate objects formally integrated into an ensemble.

Das erste Londoner Interieur von Zaha Hadid Architects in London seit zwei Jahrzehnten fordert im Erdgeschoss des renovierten georgianischen Home House Raum. Die Installationen, in gesättigten georgianischen Farben, fließen durch Bar, Eingangsbereich und Empfangsräume und bilden eine Landschaft skulpturaler Inseln aus. Die gewundenen Formen entsprechen den flüssigen Geometrien von natürlichen Systemen und Verkrümmungen. James Wyatt's Räume werden in der Funktionalität der Zusammensetzung der fließenden und neuartigen Formen wiederentdeckt. Die Inseln schwimmen zwischen Geschichte und Zukunft, laden Vergangenheit und Gegenwart, Elastizität und Solidität sowie Handwerkskunst über drei Jahrhunderte hinweg zum Dialog. Der Barraum wird vom Tresen dominiert, Mitglieder und Gäste werden Teil des Gesamtkunstwerks. In der Lounge wurde hingegen eine höheres Maß an Wärme und Intimität erreicht, indem sie als horizontal integrierendes Ensemble disparater Objekte angelegt wurde.

← Bar island. Barinsel.

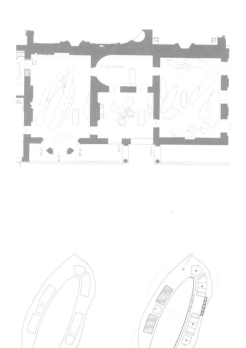

←← Side view of bar seating area. Seitenansicht des Sitzbereichs der Bar.
← Detail of dynamic island bar. Detail der dynamischen Barinsel.
↑ Floor plan and concept bar plan. Grundriss und Konzeptplan der Bar.
↙ Front view of illuminated fibre glass bar. Vorderansicht der beleuchteten Bar aus Fiberglas.

Typical of British interior design is...

the space-saving invention
and bold use of shape
and colour.

Bangalore Express

Michael Westthorp - Outline

Address: 103-105 Waterloo Road, London SE1 8UL. **Client:** Walterloo Leisure Ltd. **Completion:** 2009. **Main function:** Restaurant. **Materials:** Walnut, painted MDF.

Outline's approach to the project involved stripping the space back to its basic shell of three separate areas. Great care was taken to frame the views through and between these spaces, so that they make a cohesive whole, while maintaining a sense of intimacy. The restaurant's wall cladding has a linear pattern cut into it. This was done on site using a circular saw to make shallow grooves. The cladding was then painted one solid colour, after which some of the shapes, created by the grooves, were painted in a strict palette of three contrasting colours. This allowed a composition of shapes and colours, moving the customer's eyes around and through the spaces in a controlled way. A series of double height booths runs the entire length of one side of the restaurant. Diners access the higher seating by a scaffold tube step ladder. The booths have proved to be a popular feature of the restaurant, whilst also providing a valuable 24 extra covers.

Der Grundgedanke des Büros Outline bei diesem Projekt war, den Raum zurück zu seiner ursprünglichen Struktur von drei Bereichen zu führen. Es wurde viel Wert darauf gelegt, die Ansichten und Blickbeziehungen zwischen diesen Räumen aufzunehmen und zu rahmen, so dass die Teile ein zusammenhängendes Ganzes ergeben, und trotzdem das Gefühl von Privatheit entsteht. In die Wandverkleidung wurde auf der Baustelle mittels Kreissäge ein geometrisches Muster geritzt. Die Wand wurde vollständig in einer Farbe gestrichen, danach wurden einige der durch die Ritzen entstandenen Formen in einer Palette von drei kontrastierenden Farben gestrichen. Dadurch entstehen Formen und Farben, die die Blicke der Gäste durch die Räume lenken. An einer Seite des Restaurants wurden doppelstöckige Nischen über die gesamte Länge eingebaut. Zu den oberen Tischen gelangt man nur über die aus Rohren zusammengesetzten Leitern. Diese Nischen sind zu einer beliebten Einrichtung des Restaurants geworden, und bieten 24 zusätzliche Sitzplätze.

← Double height booths. Doppelstöckige Nischen.

↖ Main dining room. Hauptraum.
↑ Detail wall. Detail Wand.
← Detail of wall display. Detail der Wandverkleidung.
↗ Front view of double height booths. Ansicht der doppelstöckigen Nischen.
↘ Floor plan. Grundriss.
↘↘ Walnut floors and seating areas. Die Fußbodenbelag aus Walnuss-Holz geht in die Sitzbänke über.

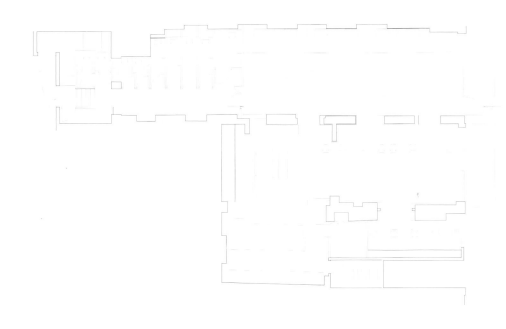

Typical of British interior design is...

the use of natural materials, cleverly executed to achieve a dynamic space.

Lucky 7 Canteen

Surface ID Ltd.

Address: 160-166 Bath Street, Glasgow, Lanarkshire G2 4TB. **Completion:** 2009. **Main function:** Restaurant / bar. **Materials:** Wood, concrete, steel, resin, distressed wallpaper and bark.

The brief was for a pared back interior with an under-designed feel that would be quirky and lived in and target both the office workers and the pre-clubbers. Finding a way of complementing the refined period detailing and proportions with the worn feel of the design was crucial to the project's success. Budget was also a key issue and Surface ID had to create several features at minimal cost, including the cast concrete lamps and graffitied log wall. The design pays particular attention to detail through the use of textures and materials including exposed wood and brickwork, mess hall benches, concrete panels, long wooden tables and distressed wallpaper which gives Lucky 7 its unique character. The finished product is both raw and inviting yet maintains a certain refined, faded elegance reminiscent of its former glory as a grand townhouse.

Das rückgebaute, nicht gestaltet scheinende Interieur der Lucky 7 Canteen zielt, mit seiner schrulligen, lebendigen Athmosphäre sowohl auf Büroangestellte als auch auf Pre-Clubber ab. Für das Entwurfskonzept des Projekts war es essentiell, kultivierte Details und Proportionen des Ursprungsinterieurs mit einem abgenutzten Charme zu verbinden. Ein strenges Budget war einzuhalten und so musste Surface ID einige Elemente, unter anderem die Betonlampen und Graffitiwände, mit geringem Kostenaufwand herstellen. Der Entwurf richtet ein besonderes Augenmerk auf Details, was in der Nutzung von verschiedenen Texturen und Materialien, einschließlich Holz und Sichtmauerwerk, von Kantinenbänken, Betonplatten, langen Holztischen und geschundenen Tapeten zum Ausdruck kommt, die dem Lucky 7 seinen einzigartigen Charakter verleihen. Das Ganze ist sowohl roh als auch einladend, wirkt durch eine raffinierte, verbliche Eleganz, die an bessere Zeiten als große Stadthaus erinnert.

← View to long wooden table and distressed wallpaper that is stylishly peeling in pales. Blick über einen langen Holztisch auf geschundene Tapeten, die sich stilvoll von der Wand schälen.

↖ Stalls at the bar with vibrant red seats. Bestuhlung der Bar mit lebendig roten Sitzflächen.

↑ Party room. Partyraum.

← Concrete lamp. Betonlampe.

↗ Sketch. Skizze.

↘ Interior general view. Totale des Innenraums.

↘↘ Detail bar. Detail der Bar.

Typical of British interior design is...
contemporary style with
a homely, almost folksy, vibe.

The Modern Pantry

Jump Studios

Address: 48 Saint John's Square, London EC1V 4JJ. **Completion:** 2008. **Main function:** Restaurant. **Lighting:** Marcel Wanders, Caravaggio and Piet Hein Eek.

The Modern Pantry, comprising upstairs and downstairs restaurant space as well as a shop/pantry, is neatly ensconced in two elegant Georgian properties. Extensive work was undertaken to convert the almost derelict buildings into a light and airy restaurant. The aim was to create an environment more akin to a domestic space than a public one. The style is contemporary with a homely, almost folksy, vibe, designed to complement Anna Hansen's culinary mission: 'to please the palate by using traditional and modern ingredients in new and exciting ways'. The glass-fronted café/restaurant is a casual dining space featuring a long rustic-style table with turned legs and Cherish chairs by Horm. The white furniture matches the dove grey colour of the walls and pillars while brickwork was deliberately left exposed to reveal a bit of history. More formal dining spaces upstairs are furnished with tables and chairs of black stained ash set against light grey walls and original wood panelling.

The Modern Pantry, mit Restaurant auf zwei Geschossen sowie einem Laden mit Teeküche, (Pantry: dt. Speisekammer, Anrichte) wurde in zwei eleganten georgianischen Gebäuden adrett inszeniert. Die nahezu verfallenen Gebäude wurden mittels umfangreicher Baumaßnahmen in ein helles und luftiges Restaurant verwandelt. Das Ziel war es, ein Umfeld zu schaffen, das eher einem privaten, denn einem öffentlichen Raum gleicht. Der Stil ist zeitgenössisch mit einer gemütlichen, fast schon volkstümlichen Stimmung, was Anna Hansens kulinarischer Mission entspricht: „Dem Gaumen durch die Verwendung traditioneller und moderner Zutaten neue und aufregende Freuden zu bieten". Das Café/Restaurant mit gläserner Front ist ein zwangloser Speisesaal mit einem langen rustikalen Tisch auf gedrechselten Beinen und den Cherish-Stühlen von Horm. Die weißen Möbel passen zu den taubengrauen Wänden und Säulen, während das Mauerwerk, als Reminiszenz an die Geschichte des Ortes, bewusst sichtbar gelassen wurde. Die förmlicheren Essräume des Obergeschosses sind mit Tischen und Stühlen aus schwarz gebeizter Esche möbliert, die sich von den hellgrauen Wänden und der erhaltenen Holzvertäfelung absetzen.

← Main dining area with long rustic-style table with turned legs.
Hauptspeiseraum mit rustikalem Tisch mit gedrechselten Beinen.

←← Brown leather banquette seating along the length of the restaurant.
Braune Lederbank an der Langseite des Restaurants.

← Copper pendant lamps by Piet Hien Eek. Hängelampen aus Kupfer von
Piet Hien Eek.

↙ Detail of dining table. Detail des Esstischs.

↓ View of Cherish chairs by Horm. Ansicht der Cherish-Stühle von Horm.

Typical of British interior design is...

the rediscovery of specifically
English traditions in their
purest contemporary form.

Haymarket Hotel

Kit Kemp

Address: 1 Suffolk Place, London SW1Y 4BP. **Landmark building designer:** John Nash. **Owner:** Firmdale Hotels. **Completion:** 2007. **Main function:** Hotel. **Materials:** Sepia-grey oak floors, stainless steel sculpture by Tony Cragg and paintings by John Virtue.

Kit Kemp has fused modern and classical references in this landmark building, which was designed by the master architect John Nash. The lobby is a clean airy space featuring a stainless steel sculpture by Tony Cragg and large black and white paintings of the London skyline. The conservatory and library have their own particular style with handpicked antiques and objects as well as original paintings by a diverse range of modern artists. The vast and impressive Shooting Gallery, 18 metres long and five meters high, has walls covered in dramatic de Gournay wallpaper featuring jungle landscapes in grey sepia tones. It is furnished with an eclectic collection of furniture including 1970s lucite tables and lamps and pictures by Oliver Messel. Downstairs, the pool area is more bar than spa. The sleek swimming pool is edged in stone, surrounded by acres of grey oak and has a ceiling covered in hundreds of fibre-optic lights. Martin Richman has installed an ever-changing colourful light installation.

Kit Kemp verbindet in diesem denkmalgeschützten Gebäude, das vom bekannten Architekten John Nash entworfen wurde, moderne und klassische Elemente. Die Lobby ist ein reduzierter, luftiger Raum mit einer Edelstahl-Skulptur von Tony Cragg und großen Gemälden der Londoner Skyline in Schwarz und Weiß. Wintergarten und Bibliothek haben mit ausgesuchten Antiquitäten und Objekten sowie Originalgemälden unterschiedlichster moderner Künstler ihren eigenen Stil. Die Wände der großen, beeindruckenden Shooting Gallery, 18 Meter lang und fünf Meter hoch, zeigen eine dramatische De Gournay Tapete mit Dschungellandschaften in Grau-Sepiatönen. Die Galerie ist mit einer divergierenden Sammlung von Möbeln bestückt, die 1970er Jahre Acrylglastische und -lampen sowie Bilder von Oliver Messel umfasst. Im Untergeschoss zeigt sich das Schwimmbad mehr als Bar, denn als Spa. Das elegante, in Stein gefasste Schwimmbecken ist von grauen Eichenfächen umgeben und wird von einer Decke mit hunderten von Glasfaserlichtern überfangen. Martin Richman trug eine ständig wechselnde, farbige Lichtinstallation bei.

← The conservatory. Der Wintergarten.

←← A bedroom in the townhouse. Ein Gästezimmer des Stadthauses.
← Private event room, Shooting Gallery. Privater Veranstaltungsraum, Shooting Gallery.
↙ Lobby. Lobby.
↓ Detail of Deluxe Double guestroom. Detail eines Deluxe Zweibett-Gästezimmers.

Typical of British interior design is...

its unconventionality. That is what makes it so unusual and dynamic.

The Cuckoo Club

Blacksheep

Address: Swallow Street, London W1B 4EZ. **Completion:** 2005. **Main function:** Bar / club. **Materials:** LED-studded dancefloor ceiling.

The Cuckoo Club is a West End venue with a difference. With a brief to appeal to London's party animals tired of fast-burn, faceless venues, The Cuckoo Club successfully married real old-school glamour to a completely modern context for a clientele that has ranged from Bryan Ferry and Robert de Niro to Kate Moss and Britain's young royals. The Cuckoo Club offers high-octane rock'n'roll glamour, with an overriding accent on comfort, fun and service. Blacksheep envisaged the club as a film set, creating a grand, dramatic, 'cigar box' fantasy house with timber cladding, huge doors, sweeping stairs, silk and voile drapes, endlessly reconfigurable LED lighting and lots of fun, original, statement design features. Every item was bespoke-designed, from the interiors concept and finishes to all the lighting design and furniture, so that the whole club has the highest possible design integrity, with the level of detailing usually preserved for the most luxurious of homes.

The Cuckoo Club im West End ist ein sehr individueller Veranstaltungsort. Der Auftrag forderte eine Gestaltung für die Londoner Party-Szene, die der gesichtslosen und flüchtigen Orte müde ist. So verbindet The Cuckoo Club erfolgreich authentischen Glamour der Alten Schule und moderne Gestaltung und spricht damit einen Kreis an, der von Bryan Ferry und Robert de Niro über Kate Moss zu Großbritanniens jungen Royals reicht. The Cuckoo Club bietet hochwertigen Rock'n'Roll-Glamour, mit Betonung auf Komfort, Spaß und Service. Blacksheep plante den Club als Filmkulisse, schuf ein großes, dramatisches Fantasiehaus mit Holzverkleidung, großen Türen, geschwungenen Treppen, Seide und Voiles, endlos rekonfigurierbarer LED-Beleuchtung und vielen verspielten und originären Design-Elementen. Jedes Element wurde passgenau gestaltet, das Gesamtkunstwerk umfasst den ganzen Raum bis hin zu jedem Detail von Beleuchtung und Möblierung, so dass ein Maß an Integrität erreicht wird, das ansonsten luxuriösesten Wohnungen vorbehalten bleibt.

← Interior view of bar. Innenansicht der Bar.

↖ The club. Der Club.
↑ Bathroom. Toiletten.
← Entrance to restaurant. Eingang des Restaurants.
↗ The snug. Die Klause.
↘ Ground floor plan. Grundriss Erdgeschoss.
↘↘ The stairwell. Das Treppenhaus.

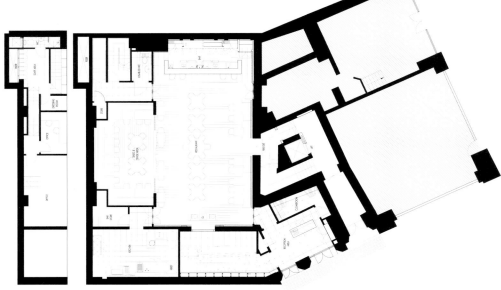

Typical of British interior design is...

striking and eclectic use of
colour, texture and pattern.

Miller of Mansfield

Ffion Sprigings

Address: High Street, Goring on Thames, Oxfordshire, RG8 9AW. **Artist:** Adam Ellis. **Client:** Wicked Varlet Ltd. **Boutique and luxury hotel specialists:** Mr & Mrs Smith. **Completion:** 2006. **Main function:** Hotel, bar and restaurant. **Materials:** Pale and black painted floorboards, bold wallpapers, bespoke refurbished antique corbeille beds, bespoke acrylic furniture and carerra marble bathrooms.

The concept at the Miller of Mansfield was to create a sexy, modern bolthole that still felt authentically 'thrown together' and eye-catchingly quirky. Throughout the design process, Ffion was working both with and to enhance the soul of the beautiful, 300 year old building. For the rooms, this meant bright colours and patterns were added to a pale background scheme. This theme followed through into the restaurant with the addition of glamorous shots of crystal, cream, button-backed banquettes and zesty, silk-taffeta blinds, catching the light, shimmering and becoming alive in the way that silk does. Something deeper and altogether murkier was needed for the bar however, to create a cosy, comfortable, warm and snug resting place for residents and locals alike.

Konzept des Miller of Mansfield ist es, einen aufreizenden modernen Unterschlupf zu schaffen, der dennoch seinen Charakter des schrulligen und offensichtlich zusammengewürfelten behielt. Während des gesamten Entwurfsprozesses versuchte Ffion die Seele des schönen, 300 Jahre alten Gebäudes sowohl zu erhalten als auch aufzuwerten. Dafür wurden die Zimmer mit strahlenden Farben und Mustern auf blassem Hintergrund aufgefrischt. Auch im Restaurant wurde dieses Konzept beibehalten, jedoch erweitert um glamouröses Kristall, Knopfpolster-Bänke und entzückende Seiden-Taft-Jalousien, die das Licht einfangen, schimmern und lebendig werden, wie es nur Seide kann. Die Bar wurde etwas dunkler und trüber gestaltet, um einen gemütlichen, komfortablen und behaglichen Ruhepunkt für sowohl Gäste als auch Einheimische zu schaffen.

← Superior double room with striking black, white and tan wallpaper.
Superior Doppelzimmer mit bestechender schwarz-weiß-brauner Tapete.

↖ Room 8 with antique king size bed reupholstered in lush red and pink velvet. Antikes King Size-Bett, aufgepolstert in üppigem roten und rosa Samt

↑ Bar / living room with open wood-burning fireplace. Bar und Aufenthaltsraum mit offenem Kamin.

← En-suite marble bathroom. Zimmereigenes Bad in Marmor.

↗ Standard double room with decadent black leather sleigh bed, Cole & Son wallpaper and antique armoire. Standard Einzelzimmer mit dekadentem schwarzem Leder-Bett, Cole & Son Tapete und antikem Kleiderschrank.

↘ Interior illustration. Skizze.

↘↘ Bedside table in superior double room. Nachttisch im Superior Doppelzimmer.

Typical of British interior design is...

diversity of styles and influences.

Electric Birdcage

Shaun Clarkson ID

Address: 11 Haymarket, London SW1Y 4BP. **Completion:** 2008. **Client:** Electra Leisure. **Main function:** Bar and restaurant. **Materials:** Fluorescent pink stucco ceilings, Fibonacci chequer board floors and walls and stained glass windows.

Electric Birdcage, an edgy, fantasy space hidden inside an old bank, is a surreal world of giant black polymer panthers, imposing black stallions and a merry-go-round bar. Fluorescent pink stucco ceilings and giant hand seats combine with neon wicker furniture and root tables scattered across a distorted Fibonacci chequerboard floor, which extends up the walls. Iron birdcage chandeliers dangle from the pink ceiling and the DJ himself is housed in a birdcage. Stained glass windows and dim sum add to the bizarre world of the Electric Birdcage. The extravagant interior, fusing sophisticated party venue, funhouse and late-night cocktail bar demands a reaction. With a capacity of 300, Pan-Asian food served all day and cocktails served all night by staff in retro airline dress, Electric Birdcage represents an experimental foray into an eccentric new world of interior design.

Electric Birdcage, ein widerspenstiger Fantasieraum innerhalb eines alten Bankhauses, bietet eine surreale Welt mit riesigen schwarzen Polymerpanthern, imposanten schwarzen Hengsten und einer Karussell-Bar. Fluoreszierende pinkfarbene Stuckdecken und Sitze geformt wie riesige Hände finden mit neonfarbenen Korbmöbeln und Wurzeltischen auf einem Boden mit Fibonacci verzerrtem Schachbrettmuster, das die Wände hinaufreicht, zusammen. Eiserne Vogelkäfigleuchter hängen von der rosafarbenen Decke und der DJ selbst findet sich in einem Vogelkäfig wieder. Farbige Glasfenster und gedämpftes Licht tragen ihren Teil zu der bizarren Welt des Electric Birdcage bei. Das extravagante Interieur verbindet anspruchsvollen Partyraum, Spiegelkabinett und Late-Night-Cocktail-Bar fordert vom Gast eine Reaktion. Tagsüber wird von Personal in Retro-Fluggesellschaft-Kleidung für bis zu 300 Gäste pan-asiatische Küche serviert, die ganze Nacht hindurch werden Cocktails gereicht. Das Electric Birdcage ist ein experimenteller Ausflug in eine exzentrische neue Welt der Innenraumgestaltung.

← View to main bar. Ansicht der Hauptbar.

↖ Hallway with seating areas. Flur mit Sitzbereich.
↑ Wall display with colourful birdcages. Vitrine mit bunten Vogelkäfigen.
← Backroom with stained glass windows. Hinterzimmer mit Buntglasscheiben.
↗ View to carousel bar. Ansicht der Karussell-Bar.
↘ Floor plan. Grundriss.
↘↘ Entrance way. Eingangsbereich.

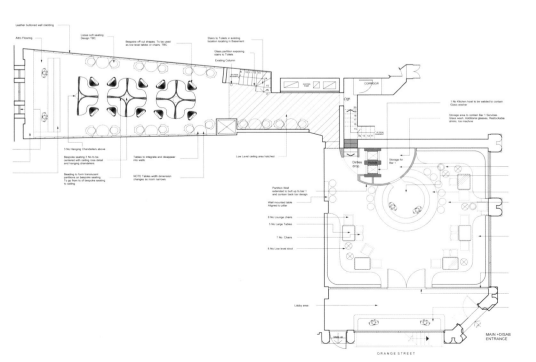

Typical of British interior design is...
an eccentric aesthetic with bold colours and modern shapes.

Knightsbridge Hotel

Kit Kemp

Address: 10 Beaufort Gardens, London SW3 1PT. **Owner:** Firmdale Hotels. **Completion:** 2002. **Main function:** Hotel. **Materials:** Chintz, tweed fabrics, floral wallpaper, plump Chesterfields, rich colour schemes, carpet and wood panelling.

Knightsbridge Hotel comprises 44 bedrooms and suites decorated by owner/designer Kit Kemp. The style is "fresh, modern English". Every room has its own individual design scheme that varies from clean neutrals to more dramatic bold colours. The bathrooms are in solid granite and oak with deep cast iron baths. The drawing room has an African feel and is designed in earthy colours, whilst the library is more romantic in soft neutrals and pale pinks. There is a vast array of original art by British artists including John Illsley and Peter Clark, as well as a stunning sculpture in the lobby by Carol Sinclair. There are specially designed fabrics by Althea Wilson, quirky book-lights by Dominic Berning and specially commissioned ceramics by Katherine Cuthbert. Both the drawing room and the library have French sandstone fireplaces and there is a fully stocked honesty bar.

Das Knightsbridge Hotel bietet 44 Zimmer und Suiten, die Inhaberin und Designerin Kit Kemp selbst gestaltet hat. Der Stil ist „frisch, modern englisch". Jedes Zimmer hat ein eigenes, individuelles Designkonzept, das von reinen neutralen, bis zu dramatischeren, kräftigen Farben reicht. Die Badezimmer sind in massivem Granit und Eiche gehalten, mit tiefen Badewannen aus Gusseisen. Der Salon ist afrikanisch geprägt und mit erdigen Farben gestaltet, während die Bibliothek sich in weichen, neutralen und blassrosa Farben romantischer gibt. Es finden sich zahlreiche Originalwerke britischer Künstler wie John Illsley und Peter Clark, eine beeindruckende Skulptur von Carol Sinclair in der Lobby, eigens entworfene Stoffe, besonders von Althea Wilson, schrulligen Leselampen von Dominic Berning und Auftragskeramiken von Katherine Cuthbert. Der Salon und die Bibliothek verfügen über Kamine aus französischem Sandstein und es gibt eine komplett ausgestattete Bar mit Selbstbedienung.

← Junior Suite with the chair and fireplace. Junior Suite mit Sessel und Kamin.

← ← Oversized headboard in guestroom. Übergroßes Kopfteil eines Bettes in einem der Gästezimmer.
← Library. Bibliothek.
↙ Individually and lavishly designed guestroom. Aufwendig und individuell gestaltetes Gästezimmer.
↓ Junior Suite. Junior Suite.

Typical of British interior design is...
an unusual and daring design,
crossed with Far East kitsch.

Inamo

Blacksheep

Address: 134-136 Wardour Street, London W1F 8ZP. **Client:** Compurants. **Completion:** 2009. **Main function:** Restaurant and bar. **Materials:** Origami wall panels.

Inamo is a 310 square metre restaurant and bar, offering customers high-quality Asian fusion cuisine. It also offers a new paradigm in the way food is ordered, with menus projected onto tabletops, allowing diners to order food and beverages interactively, to change the ambience of their individual table, to play games or even to order up local information and services, such as booking a taxi. 'Cocoon' projectors are set at the same height throughout within the suspended high-gloss black ceiling. When customers sit down, white spots for plates appear along with a customisable 'e-cloth' for each table. The concept behind the restaurant was ambitious and difficult to implement; great consideration was given especially to the lighting levels and proportions to enable the restaurant to function throughout the day and night. It was also vital that the design had an overall strong sense of identity as a space, neither overwhelming nor being overwhelmed by the technology at its heart.

Das 310 Quadratmeter große Restaurant Inamo bietet seinen Kunden hochwertige asiatische Fusion-Küche. Es läutet auch in der Art, wie die Speisen bestellt werden, eine neue Ära ein: Die Menüs werden auf die Tischplatten projiziert, so dass Gäste Speisen und Getränke interaktiv bestellen können. Zudem kann jeder Tisch und somit das Ambiente individualisiert werden. Auf ihm Spiele zu spielen oder Informationen und Dienstleistungen abzurufen, beispielsweise ein Taxi zu bestellen, ist möglich. An der abgehängten, hochglänzend schwarzen Decke befinden sich Projektoren, die weiße Kreise an Stelle der Teller und eine Auswahl elektronischer Muster anstatt Tischdecken anzeigen, sobald sich ein Gast setzt. Dieses ehrgeizige Restaurantkonzept war schwer zu realisieren, insbesondere weil Beleuchtungsstärken für Tag und Nacht ermittelt werden mussten. Ebenso wichtig war es, dem Raum als ganzes Identität zu verleihen, ohne dass Technik und Ambiente einander erdrücken.

← Private dining room. Separee.

↖ Detail of table projection. Detail der Tischprojektion.
↑ Dining table. Esstisch.
← Detail of dividing wall screen. Detail eines Raumteilers.
↗ Main dining area. Hauptspeiseraum.
↘ Ground floor plan. Grundriss Erdgeschoss.
↘↘ Bar mirror detail. Detail Spiegel an der Bar.

Typical of British interior design is...
re-inventing the traditional English inn.

The Olde Bell Inn

Ilse Crawford, Studioilse

Address: High Street, Hurley, Berkshire SL6 5LX. **Boutique and luxury hotel specialists:** Mr & Mrs Smith. **Completion:** 2008. **Main function:** Hotel. **Materials:** Rush matting, crooked floors, nooks and crannies.

With parts of the inn dating back to 1135, The Olde Bell is steeped in history. Rather than sacrificing its oak-beamed medieval heritage, Ilse Crawford chose rather to re-invent it and imbue the interior with a rustic elegance that is still quintessentially English. Chunky farmhouse furniture, oak floorboards, woven wool blankets and natural tones combine to create a cosy, comfortable feel to what is also a strikingly modern interior. Hand-made rush matting even adds a grassy rustic aroma to the rooms. The bathrooms are fitted with drench showers and elegant claw-foot baths. The rooms themselves do not dominate The Olde Bell Inn; rather it is the common spaces that are the heartbeat of the hotel which functions almost like a village in itself. While the main building provides space for the overnight guests and locals, auxiliary buildings are available for private gatherings.

In Teilen auf das Jahr 1135 zurückgehend, ist die Pension The Olde Bell ein geschichtsträchtiger Ort. Ilse Crawford entschloss sich, den mittelalterlichen Bestand der Eichen-Balken nicht zu opfern, sondern mit ihnen ein Interieur rustikaler Eleganz, wie es immer noch typisch englisch ist, neu zu erfinden. Stämmige Bauernmöbel, Eichendielen, gewebte Wolldecken und natürliche Farbtöne verbinden sich zu einem sowohl gemütlichen als auch modernen Interieur, in dem man sich wohl fühlt. Die handgemachten Binsenmatten fügen den Zimmern obendrein eine Grasnote hinzu. Die Badezimmer haben Duschen und elegante Klauenfuß-Wannen. Die Zimmer dominieren The Olde Bell Inn jedoch nicht, vielmehr sind es die Gemeinschaftsräume, die das Herzstück des Hotels bilden und seine Funktion – einem Dorf ähnlich – ausmachen. Das Hauptgebäude bietet den Übernachtungsgästen und Einheimischen Raum, während die Nebengebäude für private Veranstaltungen zur Verfügung stehen.

← Inn Suite. Inn Suite.

↖ Bathroom. Badezimmer.
↑ Event space. Veranstaltungsraum.
← Wedding salon. Hochzeitssalon.
↗ Inn Suite. Inn Suite.
↘↘ Inn Double. Doppelzimmer.

momentary disorientation to aesthetical surprise.

Olivomare

Pierluigi Piu

Address: 10 Lower Belgrave Street, London SW1W. **Client:** Mauro Sanna. **Completion:** 2007. **Main function:** Restaurant. **Materials:** Wall clad in an M.C. Escher inspired pattern, laminated plastic, resin floor and Corian counter.

Olivomare is a seafood restaurant belonging to the well-known London brand "Olivo". The formal and decorative language of the interior highlights its function with overt references to the sea environment. The most explicit among them is undoubtedly the wide wall that dominates the main dining room, entirely covered by cladding featuring a pattern inspired by the works of Maurits Cornelis Escher, in which each single portion of colour is laser cut out of a sheet of opaque laminated plastic before being juxtaposed on the vertical surface as if part of a vast jigsaw puzzle. As a contrast in the same room, a linear sequence of tubular luminescent "tentacles", spirals and twists of tubular nylon mesh drops down from the ceiling, evoking a stray shoal of jellyfish, while a mesh of fishermen's nets divide this room from the entrance lobby. In the small dining room at the rear, the cladding of the curved continuous wall is characterised by a wavy relief evoking the sandy surface of a beach moulded by the wind.

Olivomare ist ein Meeresfrüchte-Restaurant der in London bekannten Marke „Olivo". Die formelle und dekorative Sprache des Interieurs unterstreicht mit deutlichen Verweisen auf die Meereswelt. Am eindringlichsten ist sicherlich der Verweis durch die große, den Hauptspeisesaal dominierende Wand, die vollständig mit einem vom Werk Maurits Cornelis Escher inspirierten Muster überzogen ist. Jedes einzelne Farbelement dieses gigantischen Puzzles wurde mit Lasern aus opaken Kunststofflaminatplatten geschnitten und dann an der Wand befestigt. Im gleichen Raum hängt als Kontrast hierzu eine lineare Folge röhrenförmiger leuchtender "Tentakel", Spiralen und Verdrehungen eines röhrenförmigen Nylonnetzes tropfenartig von der Decke herab, die das Bild eines verirrten Quallenschwarms erwecken, während die Maschen eines Fischernetzes diesen Raum von der Lobby abtrennen. Im rückwärtigen, kleinen Speisesaal beschwört das wellenförmige Relief der Verkleidung der durchgehenden, geschwungenen Wand die Erinnerung an die sandige Oberfläche eines vom Wind gekämmten Strandes herauf.

← Wallpaper with M.C. Escher inspired pattern. Tapete mit von M. C. Escher inspiriertem Muster.

↖ Interior view into different eating areas. Innenansicht mit zwei verschiedenen Essbereichen.
↑ Bathroom. Toilette.
← Eating area with rippled walls. Speiseraum mit welligen Wänden.
↗ Interior perspective. Perspektive Innenraum.
↘ Floor plan. Grundriss.
↘↘ Detail of rippled wall. Detail der welligen Wand.

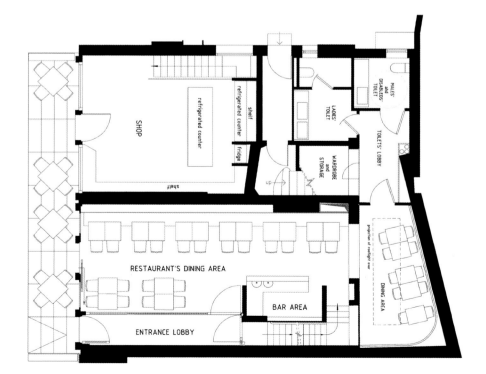

SHOP

refrigerated counter

refrigerated counter

shelf

fridge

shelf

MALES and DISABLEDS TOILET

LADIES TOILET

TOILETS LOBBY

WARDROBE and STORAGE

up

projection of rooftops area

DINING AREA

RESTAURANT'S DINING AREA

BAR AREA

ENTRANCE LOBBY

The New White Lion

JPCreative Ltd.

Address: 53 Stone Street, Llandovery Carmarthenshire SA20 OB. **Client:** Mr. and Mrs. G.S. Pritchard. **Boutique and luxury hotel specialists:** Mr & Mrs Smith. **Completion:** 2006. **Main function:** Hotel. **Materials:** Double fired wood floors, silks, recycled materials and salvaged/reclaimed artefacts.

This Grade II listed country inn has been transformed into a boutique hotel that marries fresh design with the elegance of a Georgian country house. Its six rooms, all named after a local character or legend, feature hand-selected regional materials and original furnishings and antiques that reflect an appreciation of the local heritage and culture. The Lady of the Lake room, for example, is inspired by a folklore maiden who appeared from the local Llyn y fan Fach lake and is accordingly enchanting, ethereal and calming in tone. A contemporary glass chandelier and bold accent wall covering grace the dining room, which also features original seating newly upholstered. The hotel throughout boasts a successful combination of oak, linen, welsh slate and stone, while flamboyant fabrics, silks and velvets add an element of luxury. An innate "sense of place" emanates from every corner of this inn, in which beautiful antiques and curious objects are offset by décor graced with a contemporary touch.

Der denkmalgeschützte Landgasthof wurde in ein Boutiquehotel verwandelt, das frisches Design mit der Eleganz eines georgianischen Landhauses verbindet. Die sechs Zimmer, jedes nach einer lokalen Bekanntheit oder einer Legende benannt, sind mit handverlesenen regionalen Materialien und originellen Möbeln und Antiquitäten ausgestattet, die die örtliche Kultur und Kulturgeschichte widerspiegeln. Der Lady of the Lake-Raum beispielsweise spielt auf die volkstümliche Figur eines Mädchen am Llyn y Fan Fach-See an und ist entsprechend mit bezaubernden, ätherischen und beruhigenden Farbtönen gestaltet. Ein zeitgemäßer Kronleuchter aus Glas und eine auffällige Wandverkleidung zieren den Speisesaal, dessen ursprüngliche Sitzmöbel neu gepolstert wurden. Eine gelungene Kombination aus Eiche, Leinen, walisischem Schiefer und Stein prägt das Hotel, während extravagante Stoffe, Seide und Samt, einen luxuriösen Moment hinzufügen. Der ursprüngliche „Geist des Ortes" findet sich in jeder Ecke des Gasthauses, in dem wunderschöne Antiquitäten sowie kuriose Gegenstände und ein modern anmutendes Dekor sich gegenseitig betonen.

← Living room. Wohnzimmer.

↖ View into guestroom and bathroom. William Williams Pantycelyn-Zimmer.
↑ Lounge area with fireplace. Lounge mit Kamin.
← Hallway entrance. Eingangsdiele.
↗ Lady of the Lake suite. Lady of the Lake-Suite.
↘ Lobby. Lobby.
↘↘ Honesty Bar. Honesty Bar.

LOVER

Typical of British interior design is...
a decadent and daring
theatrical mixture.

Loungelover Bar

Hassan Abdullah, Stefan Karlson and Michel Lasserre

Address: 1 Whitby Street, London E1 6JU. **Completion:** 2003. **Main function:** Bar. **Materials:** Chandeliers, antique glass tables, and eerie remnants of dismembered dolls' houses.

Loungelover is situated in a former meatpacking factory, which was stripped to its shell of bare bricks and exposed beams. The old factory skylights were then covered with films of varying blue hues and the huge glazed rear doors with red and pink film. Varying green hues of film were added to the glass partition into the kitchen. Walking into Loungelover, the visitor is immediately confronted with a colourful and lively environment, in which the sea-green feel of the kitchen and the blue of the sky complement the drama of the red area. The industrial setting became an interesting backdrop for numerous styles of furniture from the 18th to the 21st century, mainly of French, Italian, Swedish, English and Asian origins. The long building allowed different sections with varying atmospheres to be created. One such area is "the cage", the entrance to which came from the folding gate of a 19th century Parisian butcher. Another area is lined with gold wallpaper and guarded by an enormous hippo.

Loungelover befindet sich in einem ehemaligen Fabrikgebäude zur Fleischverpackung, das bis auf den Kern aus Mauerwerk und nackten Holzbalken abgebrochen wurde. Die Oberlichter der Fabrik werden durch Filme unterschiedlicher Blautöne gedämpft, die großen Glastüren der Rückseite des Gebäudes sind in Rot und Rosa abgetönt. Unterschiedliche Grünvarianten wurden für die Glaswand zur Küche genutzt. Der Besucher betritt mit dem Loungelover eine bunte und lebendige Welt, in der das Meergrün-Gefühl der Küche und das Blau des Himmels die Dramatik des roten Bereichs ergänzen. Das industrielle Ambiente wurde als interessante Kulisse für verschiedenste Möbel des 18. bis 21. Jahrhunderts, meist aus Frankreich, Italien, Schweden, England oder Asien, genutzt. Die Länge des Gebäudes ermöglichte es, verschiedene Bereiche mit ganz unterschiedlicher Atmosphäre zu schaffen. Einer dieser Bereiche ist „The Cage", dessen Eingang vom Falttor einer Pariser Metzgerei des 19. Jahrhundert stammt. Ein weiterer Bereich ist mit goldenen Tapeten ausgekleidet und wird von einem riesigen Nilpferd bewacht.

← A stag's head handcrafted with red and pink crystal as a focal point to divide the lounge sections. Ein kunstfertig mit roten und rosafarbenen Kristallen besetzter Hirschkopf dient der Teilung der Lounge.

↖ Taxidermy of a hypo's head guarding the entrance to the gold private room, a 1950 starburst crystal chandelier and Chinese porcelain vases. Ein ausgestopfter Nilpferdkopf bewacht den Eingang zum goldenen Separee, einem Sternenexplosionsluster aus Kristall der 1950er Jahre und chinesische Porzellanvasen.

↑ View to a collection of French and Swedish furniture and 17th century painted tapestry from Aubusson. Französische und Schwedische Möbel vor einem gemalten Wandteppich aus Aubusson aus dem 17. Jahrhundert.

← A square multi-coloured American Perspex wall light, a metal sign in the shape of an anchor. Eine quadratische mehrfarbige amerikanische Wandleuchte aus Plexiglas, ein Metall-Schild in Ankerform.

↗ Overall view of the room with blue sky lights, Murano chandelier from the British Embassy in Rome, sideboard cabinet to store cutlery. Gesamtansicht des Zimmers mit blauen Oberlichtern, Murano-Kronleuchter der britischen Botschaft in Rom, Büffetschrank um Besteck aufzubewahren.

↘ 17th century carved wood window frame filled with multi-coloured crystals, 19th century metal swan with original paint, 19th century French cabinet. Geschnitzter Fensterrahmen mit bunten Kristallen aus dem 17. Jahrhundert, Schwan aus Metall mit Originallackierung aus dem 19. Jahrhundert, französischer Wandschrank aus dem 19. Jahrhundert

↘↘ View to 1960 Murano chandelier and 19th century Czechoslovakian painted carousel horses. Ansicht eines Murano-Kronleuchters von 1960 und gefasster tschechoslowakischer Karussellpferde des 19. Jahrhunderts.

Typical of British interior design is...
unexpected luxury in an original 16th century farm.

Hurst House on the Marsh

de VALERO Design (Juliet de Valero Wills)

Address: East Marsh, Laugharne, Carmarthenshire, South West Wales, SA33 4RS. **Co-owner:** Neil Morrissey. **Boutique and luxury hotel specialists:** Mr & Mrs Smith. **Completion:** 2008. **Main function:** Hotel. **Materials:** Pebble-floored bathrooms, oak floors, leather armchairs.

Hidden away on the far southwestern corner of the Welsh coast, Hurst House on the Marsh is a haven of boutique luxury. Originally a 16th century dairy farm, it sits in the heart of 26 acres of marshland, but its recent overhaul by de Valero Design places Hurst House at the forefront of modern hotel interior design. 18 bedrooms and a spa located within stunningly renovated outhouses enclose a large courtyard, while the main house and restaurant overlook an organic kitchen garden and the marshland beyond. Many of the original buildings were listed, presenting a challenge to the designers who aimed to create a hotel of the highest standard of comfort and service whilst preserving the full character of the ancient structures. A new swimming pool/Jacuzzi, spa treatment area and restaurant extension formed the final and most ambitious phase of the project, which began in 2002.

Im südwestlichen Winkel der walisischen Küste gelegen, ist Hurst House on the Marsh als Boutiquehotel der Luxusklasse eine Oase. Der ursprüngliche Milchbauernhof aus dem 16. Jahrhundert, inmitten von 26 Hektar Sumpfland gelegen, stieg aufgrund der Renovierung durch Valero Design in die Spitzengruppe moderner Hotelgestaltung auf. 18 Zimmer und ein Wellnessbereich in den renovierten Nebengebäuden umschließen einen erstaunlich großen Hof. Das Haupthaus und das Restaurant überblicken einen Gemüsegarten mit organischem Anbau und das Sumpfland. Eine besondere Herausforderung für die Gestalter war, dass viele der ursprünglichen Gebäude denkmalgeschützt sind und sie deren Charakter gänzlich bewahren wollten, während zugleich ein Hotel mit höchsten Ansprüchen an Komfort und Service entstehen sollte. Das neue Schwimmbad mit Jacuzzi, ein Spa-Bereich und die Erweiterung des Restaurants stellen die letzte Bauphase des 2002 begonnenen Projekts dar.

← Suite. Suite.

↖ Suite decorated in quirky but sumptuous style. In gerissenem aber kostspieligem Stil geschmückte Suite.
↑ Mezzanine suite. Entresol-Suite.
← Sitting area. Sitzbereich.
↗ Standard suite with antique bed. Standardsuite mit antikem Bett.
↘ Lounge / bar. Lounge / Bar.
↘↘ Spiral staircase leading to a small galleried bedroom above. Wendeltreppe, die zu einem kleinen Schlafzimmer oben führt.

Typical of British interior design is...
whimsical, maximalist, with a touch of
romance, glamour and humour

Les Trois Garçons

Hassan Abdullah, Stefan Karlson and Michel Lasserre

Address: 1 Club Row, London E1 6JX. **Completion:** 2000. **Main function:** Restaurant. **Materials:** Crystal chandeliers, vintage handbags, stuffed animals perch on the bar and crane wood panelling.

The listed interiors of Les Trois Garçons, situated in a converted Victorian pub in Shoreditch, were renovated to add a sense of fun and glamour to the otherwise sombre and dark atmosphere. Photographs of the original interior guided the renovation. The mahogany bar was reinstated in its original position in the middle of the room and one of the three large eglomise mirrors advertising the house liquors was recreated using the Victorian method of acid etching, gilding and painting from the reverse side of the mirror. The crystal beaded chandeliers were specifically designed to lower the height of the high ceiling and beaded crystals were strung in long strands along the windows to glamourise and disguise the urban view. Quirky examples of Victorian taxidermy adorned with jewellery add an element of humour and fun while the redundant mahogany bar has become home to a collection of objects ranging from bronze herons and a statue of a Dalmation to porcelain cockerel casserole pots.

Das denkmalgeschützte Interieur des Les Trois Garçons, in einem umgebauten viktorianischen Pub in Shoreditch wurde so renoviert, dass Spaß und Glamour in die düstere und dunkle Atmosphäre Einzug halten. Hierzu wurde auf Fotos der ursprünglichen Ausstattung zurückgegriffen. Die Mahagoni-Bar bekam wieder ihre ursprüngliche Position in der Mitte des Raumes und einer der drei großen Spiegel mit Hinterglasmalerei die Werbung für die Liköre des Hauses machen, wurde mit der viktorianischen Technik von Säureätzung, Vergoldung und Malerei auf der Rückseite des Spiegels wiedererschaffen. Die speziell entworfenen Kristallperlen-Lüster mindern die Höhe der Decke optisch und Kristallperlen wurden in langen Ketten vor die Fenster gehängt, um das städtische Umfeld zu verschleiern und zu glorifizieren. Skurile Beispiele viktorianischer Präparationskunst zeugen von Humor, während die überflüssig gewordene Mahagoni-Bar eine Sammlung verschiedenster Objekte – vom Bronzereiher und einer Dalmatinerplastik bis hin zu Porzellantöpfen in Hahnengestalt – zur Schau stellt.

← Chimpanzee made by a French 19th century sculptor. Schimpanse eines französischen Bildhauers des 19. Jahrhunderts.

↖ Long crystal chandeliers designed by Les Trois Garçons, Murano leaf chandelier originally made for a French restaurant in Paris. Lange Kristallleuchter von Les Trois Garçons entworfen, Muranoglas Blattleuchter eines französischen Restaurants in Paris.

↑ Portrait of Les Trois Garçons presented by a friend, flanked by vintage costume jewellery. Porträt der Trois Garçons von einem Freund, flankiert von altem Kostümschmuck.

← Chef's table with a one way mirror onto the kitchen, 18th century cabinet with heart shapes cut out. Tafel mit Spionspiegel in die Küche, Kabinett des 18. Jahrhunderts mit herzförmigen Löchern.

↗ Vintage handbags hanging from the ceiling, a collection of bronze herons, porcelain Dalmation, Sicilian porcelain cockerel, Tiffany's 1940s pocket watch in the background. Alte Handtaschen hängen von der Decke, eine Sammlung bronzener Reiher, Dalmatiner aus Porzellan, sizilianischer Porellanhähne, im Hintergrund Tiffany's Taschenuhr der 1940er Jahre.

↘ Mounted giraffe's head, Marco Polo's goat, painting by Lucien Foller entitled "The Flow of Life". Ausgestopfter Giraffenkopf, Marco Polos Ziege, Lucien Foller Gemälde "Der Fluss des Lebens".

Typical of British interior design is...

emphasis on edgy glamour and individuality, whilst always maintaining home from home comfort.

Sanctum Soho Hotel

Can Do

Address: 18-22 Warwick Street, London W1B 5NF. **Client:** Concept Venues, Soho Estates. **Completion:** 2009. **Main function:** Hotel, restaurant and bar. **Materials:** Timber floors, special finishes (e.g. Armourcoat) to walls, precious papers, custom designed furniture by Can Do.

Can Do's brief was to create a luxurious, sexy rock'n'roll hotel from a conversion of two Victorian townhouses into one building in Soho. The challenge was to be playful without being kitsch and adventurous without being absurd. Can Do focused on how to make a hotel sexy and exciting from the moment a guest enters the lobby and were given the freedom to make some bold strides away from the accepted rules of hotel design. They asked questions such as, why is a desk important? Why not replace it with a cocktail bar? Various schemes were generated and given working titles during the project such as Espresso Deco, Purple Haze, Silver Bullet and Naked Luxe. Espresso Deco, for example, is a nod to the Art Deco heritage of the listed building which forms part of the hotel, and is a fabulous combination of glimmering chocolate walls, classic deco maple veneers and rich panne velvet drapes, as well as deeply sexy black bathrooms.

Can Do's Auftrag verlangte zwei viktorianische Stadthäuser in Soho in ein luxuriöses, aufreizendes Rock'n'Roll-Hotel zu verwandeln. Die Herausforderung bestand darin, es verspielt zu gestalten ohne kitschig zu werden, abenteuerlich aber nicht absurd zu wirken. Can Do konzentrierte sich darauf, das Ambiente von der Lobby an, wo der Gast das Hotel betritt, aufreizend und spannend auszubilden und erhielt alle Freiheit, sich kühn über die allgemein gültigen Regeln der Hotelgestaltung hinweg zu setzen. Sie hinterfragten wozu es einen Schreibtisch brauche? Und ob eine Cocktail-Bar ihn nicht ersetzen könne? Verschiedene Schemen mit Arbeitstiteln wie Espresso Deco, Purple Haze, Silver Bullet und Naked Luxe entstanden im Projektverlauf. Espresso Deco, zum Beispiel, ist eine Referenz an eines der in das Hotel einbezogegen, denkmalgeschützten Gebäude, das aus dem Art-Deco stammt. Es ist die fabelhafte Kombination schokoladenbraun schimmernder Wände, klassischer Ahornfurniere, prächtiger Pannesamtgardinen und aufreizender, schwarzer Badezimmer.

← Balcony Suite with satin and pale pinks including a circular bed.
Balkonsuite mit Satin in hellem Rosa und einem runden Bett.

↑ Roof garden. Dachgarten.
← Deluxe Double guestroom with work station. Arbeitsplatz in einem Deluxe Doppelzimmer.
↗ Deluxe Double guestroom with Rococo style bed. Deluxe Doppelzimmer mit Bett im Stil des Rokoko.
↘ Detail bed headboard. Detail Kopfbereich des Betts.
↘↘ View into bathroom. Blick ins Badezimmer.

Typical of British interior design is...
dramatic individual style.

The Soho Hotel

Kit Kemp

Address: 4 Richmond Mews, London W1D 3DH. **Owner:** Firmdale Hotels. **Completion:** 2004. **Main function:** Hotel. **Materials:** Taupe and bisque stripes, velvet loveseats, white matelassé bedcovers, custom faux-fleamarket dressers.

At The Soho Hotel co-owner and designer Kit Kemp has aimed for "contemporary London style", giving each of the 91 rooms and suites a different look. Some burst with colour and pattern, others are more calming and restrained. All reflect her personal attention to detail. The rooms are some of the largest to be found in London and are characterised by dramatic oversized bedheads, sleek modern furniture and bespoke lighting. The ground floor blends wood, metal, glass and stone – 12 inch oak floorboards sit alongside metal framed windows and doors, pebble lined pillars and French fireplaces. The hotel's spacious drawing room is a host of colour mostly in pinks and greens, whilst the nearby library blends warm neutrals with clean-line modern sofas and lamps. Kit Kemp's collection of modern art is clearly evident throughout. Whether it be a Peter Clark collage or a vibrant multi-coloured triptych, the art is unique. A spectacular 10 feet high bronze cat by Botero stands guard at the hotel's entrance.

Mitbesitzerin und Designerin des The Soho Hotel Kit Kemp versuchte einen „zeitgenössichen Londoner Stil" zu schaffen, indem sie die 91 Zimmer und Suiten unterschiedlich gestaltete. Einige scheinen vor Farbe und Muster fast zu platzen, andere sind ruhig und zurückhaltend, aber alle zeigen ihre Liebe zum Detail. Die Gästezimmer, die zu den größten Londons gehören, werden durch dramatisch vergrößerte Kopfteile an den Betten, schlankem modernem Mobiliar und einer gezielten Beleuchtung charakterisiert. Im Erdgeschoss verschmelzen Holz, Metall, Glas und Stahl – Dielenbretter finden sich neben metallgerahmten Fenstern und Türen, kieselsteinverkleideten Stützen und französischen Kaminen. Der großzügige Salon des Hotels ist in Rosa und Grün–Tönen gehalten, während die unweite Bibliothek neutrale warme Farben mit streng geformten Sofas und Leuchten verbindet. Kit Kemps Sammlung moderner Kunst hinterlässt überall ihre Spuren. Ob es nun eine Peter Clark-Collage ist oder ein lebendiges vielfarbiges Tryptichon, es ist eine Sammlung außergewöhnlicher Kunst. Eine spektakuläre drei Meter hohe Katze aus Bronze von Botero bewacht den Eingang des Hotels.

← Deluxe colourful guestroom. Farbiges Deluxe Gästezimmer.

↖ Deluxe double room. Deluxe Doppelzimmer.
↑ Lobby. Lobby.
← Penthouse Suite 502. Penthouse Suite 502.
↗ Penthouse 502 featuring a black sofa , and a full window. Penthouse 502 mit schwarzem Sofa und Glasfront.
↘ The Terrace Suite. Die Terrassensuite.
↘↘ Library. Bibliothek.

borrowing influences from around the world to create industrial glamour.

Carbon Bar

B3 Designers

Address: Old Quebec Street, London, W1C 1LZ. **Completion:** 2007. **Main function:** Bar. **Materials:** Concrete, brick, steel, mesh and leather.

This destination venue, at the distinctive Guoman Group hotel, features an exceptional interior inspired by industrial architecture bringing raw Shoreditch chic to the West End. A unique fusion of concrete, brick, steel, mesh and leather contrasts with outsized Chesterfields, bevelled mirrors and sketches of 21st century industrial living on the walls. The design maximises space, privacy and the ability to be seen all at once. It includes a Chain Room, with chains suspended floor to ceiling to create a semi-private function room; a Champagne Bar with a five-metre high champagne wall; a 14-metre bar created from concrete blocks; and a DJ booth unusually located above the bar and floating mezzanine. The bar's toilet walls are adorned with mock blueprints that explain how to handle 20th century tools. The ladies' washrooms ironically feature scribbled instructions on how to handle heavy-duty machinery, while the gentlemen's toilets display instructions from operating manuals for ovens, irons and household objects.

Das Ausgehziel in dem distinguierten Guoman Group Hotel bietet ein ungewöhnliches, von industrieller Architektur inspiriertes Interieur, das den groben Shoreditch Chic ins Londoner West End bringt. Eine einzigartige Mischung aus Beton, Ziegeln, Stahl, Maschendraht und Leder kontrastiert mit übergroßen Chesterfield-Sofas, abgeschrägten Spiegeln und Skizzen industriellen Lebens des 21. Jahrhunderts an den Wänden. Die Gestaltung maximiert gleichzeitig Raum, Privatsphäre und das Gesehen-Werden. Das Kettenzimmer wird durch von der Decke zum Boden hängende Ketten zu einem semi-privaten Raum. Die Champagner-Bar steht vor einer fünf Meter hohen champagnerfarbenen Wand. Es gibt eine 14 Meter lange Bar aus Betonblöcken, das DJ-Pult befindet sich an ungewöhnlicher Stelle oberhalb von Bar und Zwischengeschoss. Die WC-Wände der Bar sind mit unechten Blaupausen geschmückt, die den Umgang mit Werkzeugen des 20. Jahrhunderts erklären. Auf den Damen-Toiletten sind diese ironisch mit Gekritzel über die Bedienung von schwerer Gerätschaft versehen, während die Herren-Toiletten Anweisungen für Öfen, Bügeleisen und Haushaltgegenstände zeigen.

← VIP Chain Room. VIP Kettenraum.

↖ View from bar looking onto chain room. Blick von der Bar zum Kettenraum.
↑ Sprayed graffiti of cooking utensils in men's toilets. Graffiti von Küchengegenständen in der Männertoilette.
← View of barrel wall and a Chesterfield banquette. Ansicht der Fässerwand und eines Chesterfield-Sofas.
↗ Interior view of graffiti back wall. Ansicht einer Graffitwand.
↘ Ground floor plan. Grundriss Erdgeschoss.
↘↘ VIP mezzanine. VIP Zwischengeschoss.

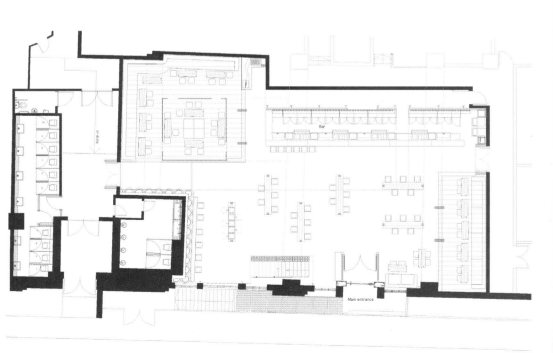

culture & leisure

Typical of British interior design is...
carving out a spatial and visual
response to the intricate relationships
of harmonies.

JS Bach Chamber Music Hall

Zaha Hadid Architects

Address: Mosley Street, Manchester M2 3JL. **Tensile structural engineer:** Tony Hogg Design. **Client:** Manchester International festival. **Completion:** 2009. **Main function:** Chamber music hall. **Materials:** Translucent fabric membrane and steel structure.

This unique chamber hall was specially designed to house solo performances of the work of Johann Sebastian Bach. A voluminous ribbon swirls within the room, carving out a spatial and visual response to the intricate relationships of Bach's harmonies. As the ribbon careens above the performer, cascades into the ground and wraps around the audience, the original room as a box is sculpted into fluid spaces swelling, merging, and slipping through one another. The ribbon consists of a translucent fabric membrane articulated by an internal steel structure suspended from the ceiling. The surface of the fabric shell undulates in a constant but changing rhythm as it is stretched over the internal structure. While enhancing the acoustic experience of the concert, the ribbon simultaneously defines a stage, an intimate enclosure, and passageways. It exists at a scale in which it is perceived as both an object floating in a room and as a temporal architecture that invites one to enter, inhabit and explore.

Dieser einzigartige Kammermusiksaal wurde speziell für Solo-Aufführungen des Werkes von Johann Sebastian Bach konzipiert. Ein voluminöses Band wirbelt durch den Raum – eine räumliche und visuelle Antwort auf die komplexen Zusammenhänge von Bachs Harmonik. Indem das Band sich über den Aufführenden hinwegschlingt, sich auf den Boden stuft und um das Publikum wickelt, verwandelt es den eckigen Raum in flüssige Räume, die ineinander fließen und miteinander verschmelzen. Das Band besteht aus einer lichtdurchlässigen Gewebe-Membran, die von einer abgehängten Stahlkonstruktion in Form gebracht wird. Über diese Innenkonstruktion wogt die Oberfläche des Gewebes in ständigem aber wechselndem Rhythmus. Sie verbessert die Akustik des Konzerterlebnisses und definiert gleichzeitig eine Bühne, einen intimen Raum und Durchgänge. Sie wirkt in zweierlei Maßstäben: als im Raum schwebender Gegenstand und als eine temporale Architektur, die einlädt wahrgenommen, betreten und erforscht zu werden.

← Voluminous ribbon swirls within the performance room. Ein dreidimensionales Band wirbelt durch den Musiksaal.

↖ Ribbon careens above the performer. Das Band, eine Schlaufe über den Interpreten ausbildend.

↑ Audience seating area. Zuschauerraum.

← Circulation delineated by the ribbon. Vom Band beschriebene Kreisform.

↗ Single continuous ribbon swirls around itself to cocoon the performers and audience. Ein einzelnes durchgehendes Band umwirbelt sich selbst, um einen Kokon um Bühne und Zuschauer auszubilden.

↘ 3D model. 3D Model.

↘↘ Detail of fabric ribbon. Gewebedetail des Bandes.

the rich internal palette of materials
within a pure external envelope.

The North Wall Arts Centre

Haworth Tompkins

Address: St. Edward's School, Woodstock Road, Oxford OX2 7NN. **Client:** St. Edward's School. **Completion:** 2006. **Main function:** Performing Arts Centre. **Materials:** Douglas fir flitched timber stained with a burnt sienna wash, aluminum and glass.

The North Wall Arts Centre houses a flexible theatre and backstage facilities within an old Victorian swimming pool and outbuildings. A new two-storey building to the east of the original pool provides a foyer/gallery, drama and dance studio. The scheme has been envisaged as a linear series of connected 'barns' built against the weathered stone boundary wall. Externally, the new building and roofscape is English Oak shingle with close oak slats at the ground floor and gables. These warm, textured surfaces are designed to mellow naturally with age and will weather to a silvery grey. The theatre space is designed as a robust, dark stained, timber galleried room within the existing brick shell. Existing high-level windows are replaced with acoustic glazing and blackout shutters. The dance studio is day-lit via a large window with an internal blackout shutter and external sliding slatted screen, and top lit from a continuous roof light along the north wall.

Das North Wall Arts Centre beherbergt ein Theater und alle dazu benötigten Einrichtungen in einem alten viktorianischen Schwimmbad und seinen Nebengebäuden. Ein neues zweigeschossiges Gebäude erweitert das Gelände und bietet ein Foyer sowie ein Tanz-Studio. Das Zentrum präsentiert sich wie eine Aneinanderreihung von „Scheunen", die in einer Reihe vor einer Steinmauer stehen. Verkleidet ist das neue Gebäude mit Eiche-Schindeln und einer engen Eiche-Lattung im Erdgeschoss. Diese warmen und strukturierten Holzoberflächen werden im Laufe der Jahre silbrig-grau verwittern. Der Zuschauersaal mit seinen rohen Ziegelwänden ist dunkel gestaltet, mit einer eingezogenen Galerie aus dunkel gefärbtem Bauholz. Die ursprünglichen hohen Fenster wurden mit Akkustik-Verglasung und Verdunkelungsmechanismen versehen. Das Tanz-Studio wird nicht nur durch ein großes Fenster mit einem innenliegenden Verdunkelungsmechanismus und außen liegenden Schiebeläden belichtet, sondern auch durch nach Norden ausgerichtete Oberlichter.

← Timber lined foyer. Mit Holz verkleideter Eingangsbereich.

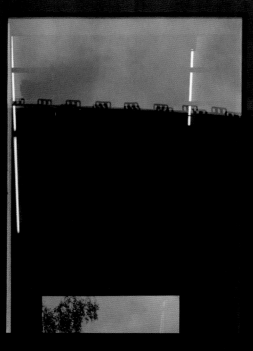

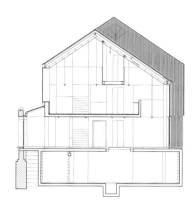

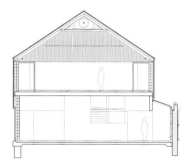

←← Oak cladded exterior. Mit Eiche verkleidete Außenfassade.
← Gallery. Foyer.
↑ Sections. Schnitte.
↙ Dance studio. Tanz-Studio.
↓ Main auditorium. Blick in den Zuschauerraum.

Typical of British interior design is...

eclecticism: a unique blend of styles,
colours and textures from a mixture
of sources and time periods.

Darwin Centre

C.F. Møller Architects

Address: Cromwell Road, London SW7 5BD. **Exhibition fitout design:** At Large. **Landscape architecture:** C.F. Møller Architects. **Completion:** 2009. **Main function:** Museum. **Materials:** Glass (façade), concrete (cocoon), natural stone (ground floor).

The second phase of the Darwin Centre is an extension of the celebrated Natural History Museum in London, taking the form of an enormous 'cocoon' in a glass enclosure. The cocoon houses the Museum's unique collections of 17 million insects and 3 million plants. Surrounding the cocoon are eight floors of offices and laboratories. As a first for the museum, the public is allowed to get behind the scenes to gain an appreciation not only of the enormous diversity and size of the collections but also of how this world resource is essential for contemporary medical and environmental research. The cocoon communicates the size, use and importance of the Natural History Museum's collections. It is constructed in sprayed concrete with a surface finish in polished plaster. Expansion joints wrap around the form, resembling silk threads. The internal and external walls of the eight-storey sun filled atrium are constructed in solar control glass. The floor in all public areas is paved with Portland stone.

Die zweite Ausbauphase des Darwin Centre, eine Erweiterung des berühmten Natural History Museum in London, entstand in Form eines riesigen "Kokons" in einem Glasbau. Der Kokon beherbergt die einzigartigen Sammlungen von 17 Millionen Insekten und 3 Millionen Pflanzen des Museums. Um den Kokon herum befinden sich acht Etagen mit Büros und Labors. Erstmals gestattet das Museum hier der Öffentlichkeit, hinter den Kulissen nicht nur einen Eindruck der enormen Vielfalt und Größe der Sammlungen zu gewinnen, sondern auch zu erkennen, welche Bedeutung diese globale Ressource für zeitgenössische medizinische und ökologische Forschung hat. Der Kokon propagiert die Größe, Nutzung und Bedeutung der Sammlung des Natural History Museums. Er ist in Spritzbeton mit einer Oberfläche aus poliertem Gips ausgeführt. An Seidenfäden erinnernde Dehnungsfugen umschließen ihn. Für die Innen- und Außenwände des achtstöckigen, sonnigen Atriums wurde Sonnenschutzglas verwendet. Der Boden aller öffentlichen Bereiche ist mit Portland-Stein gepflastert.

← View of atrium space surrounding the cocoon. Ansicht des Atriums, das den Kokon umfasst.

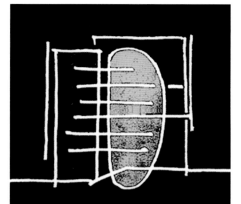

←← New bridge connecting old and new spaces. Neue Brücke, Alt- und Neubau verbindend.
← Cavernous exhibition spaces inside the cocoon. Höhlenartiger Ausstellungsraum im Kokon.
↑ Sketch concept idea and interior. Konzept- und Innenraumskizze.
↙ Cocoon expansion joints resemble silk threads. Die Dehnungsfugen des Kokons erinnern an Seidenfäden.
↓ The cocoon and surrounding laboratories. Der Kokon umgeben von Laboratorien.

Typical of British interior design is...

the layering of stories in a material narrative drawn from the physical and cultural life of a building.

Raven Row

6a Architects

Address: 56 Artillery Lane, London E1 7LS. **Client:** Alex Sainsbury. **Completion:** 2009. **Main function:** Exhibition centre. **Materials:** Aged timber boards, high pigment paint white walls, rough finish sand cast iron balustrade and ironmongery.

Raven Row, a new contemporary art exhibition centre, is embedded in two of the finest 18th century silk mercers' houses and a 1972 concrete framed office building in Spitalfields. Originally built in 1754 the Grade I listed buildings have been added to, converted, neglected, ravaged by fires and repaired over two and a half centuries. The latest intervention by 6a Architects weaves through the buildings to create a new architectural narrative of spaces, surfaces and textures that binds the past with the new in a contemporary whole. The project includes contemporary art galleries within a new semi-basement and a series of 18th century Rococo rooms over three storeys with additional studio space, offices and apartments for artists in residence above.

Raven Row, ein neues Ausstellungzentrum zeitgenössischer Kunst, ist in zwei der bedeutendsten Seidenhändlerhäuser des 18. Jahrhunderts und einem Betonbürogebäude von 1972 in Spitalfields eingezogen. Die denkmalgeschützten Seidenhändlerhäuser wurden 1754 erbaut und im Laufe von mehr als zweieinhalb Jahrhunderten umgenutzt, vernachlässigt, von Bränden verwüstet und wieder hergerichtet. Die jüngste Intervention von 6a Architects schlängelt sich als neue Geschichte von architektonischen Räumen, Oberflächen und Texturen durch die Gebäude und verbindet Vergangenheit und Neues zu einem zeitgenössischen Ganzen. Das Projekt umfasst die Galerien für zeitgenössische Kunst in einem neuen Tiefparterre sowie eine Reihe von Rokoko Zimmern aus dem 18. Jahrhundert auf drei Etagen mit zusätzlichem Atelierraum, Büros und im oberen Bereich Künstlerwohnungen.

← View into new gallery spaces. Blick in die neuen Galerieräume.

↖ Rear cast iron cladding and galleries within. Rückwärtige Gusseisenverkleidung mit Galerien.
↑ Cast iron detail ventilation. Gusseisendetails der Belüftung.
← Central contemporary gallery. Zentrale zeitgenössische Galerie.
↗ Interior view of first floor room. Innenansicht eines Zimmers im ersten Stock.
↘ Floor plans. Grundrisse.
↘↘ Interior with cast iron door knobs. Interieur mit gusseisernen Türgriffen.

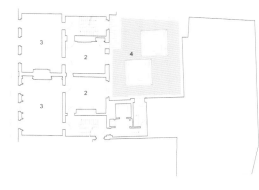

an evocative and inspiring combination of environmentally-friendly materials.

National Assembly for Wales

Richard Rogers Partnership

Address: Pierhead Street, Cardiff CF10 4JY. **Client:** National Assembly for Wales. **Completion:** 2005. **Main function:** Office. **Materials:** Rough slate, smooth concrete, steel, glass and timber.

This transparent building built for the new Welsh Assembly embodies the democratic values of participation and openness. It has an open aspect over Cardiff Bay to the Bristol Channel. The dramatic roof form is drawn down to define the 60-seat Debating Chamber, a large, circular space at the heart of the building. A slate-clad plinth steps up from the water level and is cut away, allowing daylight to enter the administrative spaces at lower levels. The building also accommodates committee and meeting rooms, press facilities, exhibition and education spaces, offices for the principal officers, a members' lounge and a café. Not only is the building architecturally progressive, but its environmental policy sets a new standard. Heat exchangers exploit the potential of the ground as a cooling mechanism, while the thermal mass of the plinth controls fluctuations in the building's internal environment.

Das transparente Gebäude für die walisische Volksvertretung verkörpert die demokratischen Werte der Partizipation und Offenheit. Das transparente Bauwerk erhebt sich über die Bucht von Cardiff und den Bristolkanal. Die dramatische Dachform zieht sich zum Plenarsaal mit sechzig Plätzen hinab, einem großen, runden Raum im Zentrum des Gebäudes. Der mit Schiefer verkleidete Sockel treppt sich vom Wasser zum Gebäude auf, Einschnittte gewährleisten die natürliche Belichtung der Verwaltungsräume auf den unteren Ebenen. Das Gebäude umfasst zudem Ausschuss- und Tagungsräume, Presseeinrichtungen, Ausstellungs- und Bildungsräumlichkeiten, Büros für die leitenden Angestellten, eine Mitglieder-Lounge und ein Café. Das Bauwerk ist nicht allein architektonisch wegweisend, sondern setzt auch umweltpolitisch neue Maßstäbe. Wärmetauscher nutzen das Kühlungspotenzial des Bodens, während die thermische Masse des Sockels Schwankungen im Gebäude ausgleicht.

← Undulating roof sheltering both internal and external spaces.
Onduliertes Dach über Innen- und Außenräumen.

↑ The wood-panelled funnel leading to the debating chamber on the mezzanine level. Café und Ausstellungsbereich.

← The inside of the funnel enhances the daylight entering into the Debating Chamber to reduce the need for artificial lighting. Windtrichter zur Belichtung und Belüftung des Plenarsaals.

↗ The reception area provides a large open space. Öffentlicher Empfangsbereich und Information.

↘ Sections. Schnitte.

↘↘ Detail of undulating wooden roof. Detail des gewölbten Daches.

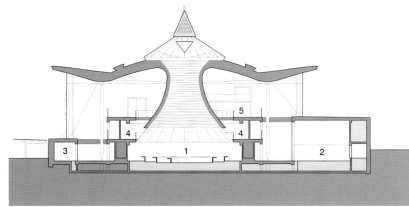

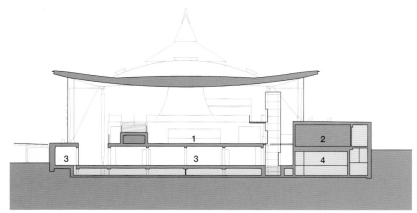

Typical of British interior design is...

architectural imagination over budgetary constraints.

The Garden Museum

Dow Jones Architects Ltd.

Address: Lambeth Palace Road, London SE1 7LB. **Completion:** 2009. **Main function:** Museum. **Materials:** Prefabricated structural timber.

The brief for the redesign of the museum asked for a new gallery space where temporary exhibitions could be housed in secure and environmentally controlled conditions. In addition, the designers created a dedicated place for the museum's permanent collection, which was previously often displaced by temporary exhibitions. A belvedere within the existing building houses the temporary gallery on the ground floor and the permanent collection on the first. This arrangement empties the nave of exhibits, enabling the museum's diverse cultural programme of lectures and debates to take place alongside the exhibitions. The belvedere is a freestanding structure made of Eurban, a pre-fabricated and lightweight but very strong timber material. The timber walls are left unfinished and recede into the background, allowing the exhibits to dominate the interior space, while the windows and doors are strongly coloured and protrude through the raw timber. Strongly coloured furniture adds a further layer of detail to the mute timber form.

Aufgabe bei der Neugestaltung des Museums war es, neuen Ausstellungsraum zu schaffen, in dem Wechselausstellungen unter kontrollierten Klimabedingungen stattfinden können. Zusätzlich schufen die Gestalter den Bereich der Dauerausstellung neu, die bislang oft temporären Ausstellungen weichen musste. Ein Belvedere, das sich in die bestehende Struktur einfügt, beherbergt nun den Wechselausstellungsbereich im Erdgeschoss und die ständige Sammlung im Obergeschoss. Diese Anordnung befreit das Kirchenschiff von Exponaten, so dass das vielfältige kulturelle Programm des Museums mit Vorträgen und Debatten neben den Ausstellungen Platz findet. Das Belvedere ist eine freistehende Struktur aus Eurban, einem vorgefertigten, leichten aber stabilen Holzwerkstoff. Die Holzwände sind unbearbeitet, so dass sie in den Hintergrund treten und die Exponate im Innenraum deutlich dominieren. Fenster und Türen sind hingegen intensiv gefärbt und heben sich so vom rohen Holz ab. Ein weitere Ebene tritt in Form des intensiv gefärbten Mobiliars vor das zurückhaltende Holzvolumen.

← Entrance area. Eingangsbereich.

↖ First floor education room. Seminarraum im ersten Obergeschoss.
↑ View across nave into meeting room. Blick durch das Schiff in den Konferentraum.
← View from the nave. Blick aus dem Schiff.
↗ Timber intervention into threading through the existing space. Hölzerne Einbauten fügen sich in den bestehenden Raum ein.
↘ Floor plan. Grundriss.
↘↘ Detail of staircase. Detail der Treppe.

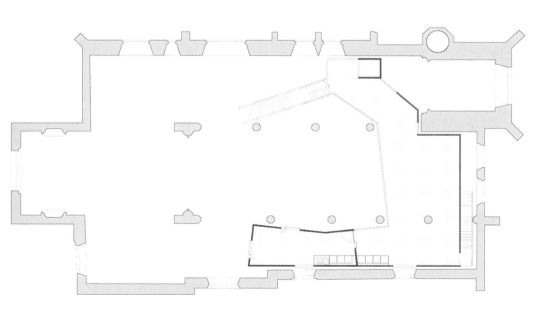

Typical of British interior design is...

idiosyncracy, its form and materials
inspired by elements of the Welsh landscape
and by the country's social, industrial and
cultural traditions.

Wales Millennium Centre

Capita Architecture

Address: Cardiff Bay, Cardiff CF10 5AL. **Client:** SRM - Roger Spence. **Structural Engineers :** Arup Cardiff - Chris Jofeh, Gabriel Hyde. **Completion:** 2009. **Main function:** Theatre, bar and restaurant. **Materials:** Wood, slate, Rimex metal and moulded plaster.

The Wales Millennium Centre was to be a landmark building befitting its location, cultural importance, and its status as a Millennium project. The design of the building draws on references from the industrial archaeology, geology and heritage of Wales. Its simple composition and limited palette of materials disguise a complexity of internal organisation. The Theatre at the heart of the project presented the greatest challenge: it was to be both a beautiful room and excellent acoustically. An all-enveloping single perimeter skin unifies the space and places the audience on 'floating' tiers within a single volume. The seating balconies were treated as physically disconnected from the walls and appear to grow out of the shaft formed by the technical control rooms at the back of the auditorium, like boughs growing away from the trunk of a tree. The balcony fronts have variegated hardwood strips, laid in horizontal strata and tailored to meet acoustic requirements.

Das Wales Millennium Centre sollte seiner Lage, kulturellen Bedeutung und dem Status als Millennium-Projekt gemäß auch architektonisch ein Wahrzeichen werden. Der Entwurf referiert auf Elemente der Industrie-Archäologie, der Geologie und des walisischen Erbes. Die einfache Komposition und eine begrenzte Palette von Materialien kaschieren die Komplexität der internen Organisation. Das Theater im Zentrum des Projektes stellte die größte Herausforderung dar: Es sollte sowohl ein schöner Raum sein als auch ausgezeichnete Akustik bieten. Eine alles umhüllende Haut fasst den gesamten Raum zu einem Volumen zusammen, in dem sich die Zuschauer auf „schwebenden" Rängen wiederfinden. Die Balkone wurden als physisch von den Wänden getrennt behandelt und scheinen wie Äste aus dem Stamm eines Baumes von den Technikräumen an der Rückseite des Auditoriums zu wachsen. Die Fronten der Balkone bestehen aus vielfarbigen Hartholz-Streifen in horizontalen Schichten und sind auf die akustischen Anforderungen zugeschnitten.

← Lobby. Lobby.

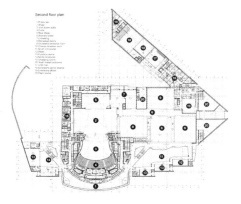

←← Auditorium. Innenraum Theater.
← Staircase lined with cedar wood. Treppenhaus mit Zederholzverschalung.
↑ Exploded 3D and floor plan. Dreidimensionale Darstellung und Grundriss.
↙ View into different levels. Blick in verschiedene Ebenen.
↓ Seating area. Sitzbereich.

home & living

Typical of British interior design is...

creating new uses for forgotten buildings while retaining the essential character and patina of the original structure.

Collage House

Jonathan Tuckey Design

Address: Paramount, Kilburn Lane, London W10. **Client:** Jonathan Tuckey. **Completion:** 2008. **Main function:** Living. **Materials:** Brick, wood and glass.

The brief was to create a family home from a former steel workshop and retain the character of the existing buildings on the long, linear site. The solution maximises the space provided by the existing buildings and only a protruding entrance box on the narrow street front suggests what lies behind. The first space is a top-lit, double height living room, beyond which the main space of the workshop has been retained as the kitchen with a black concrete floor and utilitarian worksurfaces. The outermost buildings were demolished to form a garden courtyard, enclosed on two sides by the bedrooms, creating a fluid balance of inside and outside spaces. Simple and ordinary materials were utilised to blend with the existing building and context, including features such as copper spouts and garden taps for the kitchen, exposed 'studwork' walls and a purpose-made enamelled kitchen worktop, creating a utilitarian but playful aesthetic. The layout too is informal and open, complementing the existing building.

Der Auftrag lautete, eine ehemalige Stahlwerkstatt in das zeitgenössische Heim einer Familie zu verwandeln, dabei jedoch den Charakter der bestehenden Gebäude auf dem langgestreckten Grundstück zu erhalten. Der vorhandene Raum der Altbauten wurde maximiert und lediglich ein vorspringender Eingangsbaukörper an der engen Straße kam hinzu und verrät die dahinter liegende neue Funktion. Der erste Raum ist ein durch die Decke belichtetes, zweigeschossiges Wohnzimmer, darauf folgt der ehemalige Hauptraum der Werkstatt, der bereits einen schwarzen Betonboden und funktionale Arbeitsplatten aufwies und zur Küche umgenutzt wurde. Die äußeren Gebäude wurden zugunsten eines Gartens in einem von Zimmern flankierten Innenhof abgerissen, wodurch ein fließendes Gleichgewicht von Innen- und Außenräumen entstand. Im Einklang mit den bestehenden Gebäuden und dem Kontext wurden einfache und gewöhnliche Materialien verwendet, darunter Kupferrohre und Gartenarmaturen in der Küche, rohe Pfostenwände und eine speziell gefertigte emaillierte Küchenarbeitsplatte. Auch der Grundriss ist informell und offen gestaltet.

← Kitchen / dining room in the newly remodelled steel workshop. Küche mit Esszimmer in der neuen gestalteten Stahlwerkstatt.

←← Living room with fireplace. Wohnzimmer mit Kamin.
← Kitchen with exposed brick wall and suspended copper water taps. Küche mit unverputzer Backsteinwand und freiliegenden kupfernen Wasserinstallation.
↑ Axonometric. Axonometrie.
↙ Living room with wooden resting 'box'. Wohnzimmer mit offener Ruhezone.
↓ Kitchen with exposed wooden rafters and lightwell. Küche mit sichtbaren Holzbalken und Lichthof.

Typical of British interior design is...

moody, vibrant, eclectic with a modern twist.

The Apartment, 1 Club Row

Hassan Abdullah

Address: 1 Club Row, London E1 6JX. **Completion:** 2000. **Main function:** Living. **Materials:** Black granite (bathroom), antique and designer furniture pieces.

Each area in this eclectic flat above Les Trois Garçons restaurant has its own distinctive style. The living room houses a collection of furniture from the 17th to the 21st centuries while the television area is in a 20th century style with a De Sede modular sofa as the focal point. The walls in this room are painted crimson pink, burnt orange and deep red, inspired by a collection by Yves Saint Laurent and contrasting starkly with the entirely black library. The first bedroom is French in style with a mix of Swedish furniture, the second more English with a Queen Anne four-poster bed, and the third has a sunburst theme painted in midnight blue. The dressing room is made in solid oak to reflect an English gentlemen's outfitters. The central concept of the flat was to provide an eclectic mix of spaces, each one to complement a different mood. The existing listed structure, derelict and stripped by squatters, was carefully restored with all its original details such as the cornicing and ceiling roses.

Jeder Bereich dieser eklektizistischen Wohnung über dem Restaurant Les Trois Garçons hat seinen eigenen unverwechselbaren Stil. Das Wohnzimmer verfügt über eine Sammlung von Möbeln aus dem 17. bis 21. Jahrhunderts, während der TV-Bereich sich im Stil des 20. Jahrhunderts mit einem modularen de Sede-Sofa als Zentrum zeigt. Die Wände sind in diesem Raum von einer Yves Saint Laurent-Kollektion inspiriert, purpurrosa, dunkel-orange und tief rot und kontrastieren stark mit der ganz schwarzen Bibliothek. Das erste Schlafzimmer zeigt sich französisch mit schwedischen Möbeln, das zweite mit einem Queen-Anne-Himmelbett englisch und das dritte gibt sich dunkelblau gestrichen ganz dem Thema Sonnenstrahlen. Die Garderobe aus massiver Eiche reflektiert das Erscheinungsbild eines typischen englischen Herrenausstatters. Die Idee war es, die Wohnung als Konglomerat von Räumen für unterschiedliche Stimmungen erscheinen zu lassen. Die denkmalgeschützte Substanz, verfallen und durch Hausbesetzungen des Dekors beraubt, wurde sorgfältig mit all ihren ursprünglichen Details wie den Stuckverzierungen und Rosetten restauriert.

← Bathroom made with black granite with Hansgrohe, Philippe Starck and Villeroy & Boch bathroom fittings. Badezimmer mit schwarzem Granit und Ausstattung von Hansgrohe, Philippe Starck sowie Villeroy & Boch.

↖ French style bedroom with a collection of corals, 18th century Swedish table, a beaded parrot lamp. Französisches Schlafzimmer mit einer Korallensammlung, einem schwedischen Tisch des 18. Jahrhunderts und einer Lampe mit perlenbesetztem Papagei.

↑ Early 19th century oval gilded mirror, a very large mercury ball, a 19th century wing back armchair. Vergoldeter, ovaler Spiegel des frühen 19. Jahrhunderts, ein großer Quecksilberball, ein Sessel des 19. Jahrhunderts. ← Writing desk by Jules Leleu, chandelier designed by Les Trois Garçons made of broken milk and water bottles. Schreibtisch von Jules Leleu, Kronleuchter aus zerbrochenen Milch- und Wasserflachen, entworfen von Les Trois Garçons.

↗ Jack the parrot living in a Victorian birdcage overlooking a modular sofa from De Sede, cornices made with broken pieces of mirrors and jewellery and crystals. Der Papagei Jack lebt in einem viktorianischen Vogelkäfig mit Blick auf ein modulares Sofa von de Sede, Gesimse mit Bruchstücken von Spiegeln, Schmuck und Kristallen.

↘ Perspex and metal chair by Christian Daninos (1969), 18th century stone balustrade, a pair of Arabic mirrors from the Savoy family in Italy. Plexiglas und Metall-Stuhl von Christian Daninos (1969), steinerne Balustrade aus dem 18. Jahrhundert, ein Paar arabischer Spiegel von der Savoyer Familie in Italien.

↘↘ Black lacquered library inspired by the 19th century painting of a lawyer, a pair of mirrored guitars from the 1950s, a garden ornament of a stone seahorse, 17th century cherubs. Schwarze Bibliothek inspiriert durch ein Gemälde des 19. Jahrhunderts von einem Rechtsanwalt, Spiegelgitarren aus den 1950er Jahren, ein in Gärten gebräuchliches steinernes Seepferdchen, Putten aus dem 17. Jahrhundert.

Typical of British interior design is...

fearless synthesis of disparate elements to create an uncanny, harmonious whole.

Hearth House

AOC

Address: Helenslea Avenue, London NW11 8ND. **Contractor:** John Perkins Projects. **Structural engineer:** Engineers HRW. **Concrete consultant:** David Bennett. **Completion:** 2009. **Main function:** Living. **Materials:** Reclaimed hardwood, in-situ concrete, plywood and plasterboard.

The Hearth House is a redeveloped Edwardian semi-detached house in North London that provides a new home for a family of five. Untouched since the 1940s the old house enjoyed a generous provision of space but was dark, spatially unvaried and saturated in the residue of the previous residents. The new house has a range of differing spaces, whose individual characters are defined through a variety of architectural effects. A triple height space, lit from above by an operable roof light, brings direct sunlight into the north-facing spaces. At its base a warm poured concrete hearth and stair provide a centre for family life, perfect for clambering and reclining. The pattern of the reclaimed chevron parquet flooring is repeated in the surface of the concrete, encouraging domestic and historical associations. Nooks, internal windows and screens ensure the family can easily enjoy the more public areas of the house whilst maintaining their own desired level of privacy.

Das Hearth House ist eine sanierte edwardianische Doppelhaushälfte in Nord-London, die einer fünfköpfigen Familie ein neues Zuhause bietet. Seit den 1940er Jahren unverändert, bot das alte Haus zwar großzügige Räume, war aber auch dunkel, räumlich unverändert und von früheren Bewohnern heruntergewohnt. Der Umbau bietet nun ganz unterschiedliche Zimmer, deren einzelne Charaktere durch eine breite Palette architektonischer Effekte entstehen. Ein Raum der sich über drei Geschosse erstreckt, lässt durch ein verstellbares Oberlicht direktes Sonnenlicht in die nach Norden gerichtete Räume. An seinem Fuß bieten ein wärmender Ofen aus Gussbeton und Treppenstufen der Familie ein Zentrum, das sich ideal zum Klettern und Anlehnen eignet. Das Muster der wiederhergestellten Chevron-Parkettböden wiederholt sich in der Oberfläche des Betons und weckt heimatliche und historische Assoziationen. Ecken, innenliegende Fenster und Schirmwände gewährleisten, dass die Familie die öffentlicheren Bereiches des Hauses genießen und sich in graduell privatere Bereiche zurückziehen kann.

← Dining room with fireplace. Esszimmer mit Kamin.

VASARELY
MÚZEUM

H-7621 Pécs, Káptalan utca. 3.

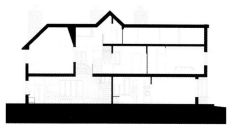

←← Stair dividing at the first floor landing. Treppen am Treppenabsatz.
← The in-situ concrete hearth and heated bench. Ortbetonofen und Ofenbank.
↑ Ground floor plan and section. Grundriss Erdgeschoss und Schnitt.
↙ Double sided fireplace with office beyond. Zweiseitig zugänglicher Kamin mit dahinterliegendem Büroraum.
↓ View upwards to sculptural staircase. Blick in das skulpturale Treppenhaus.

elegance and simplicity.

Sunken House

Adjaye Associates

Address: 75A De Beauvoir Road, London N1 4EZ. **Client:** Ed Reeve. **Completion:** 2007. **Main function:** Living. **Materials:** Solid spruce cross laminated panel superstructure, black stained cedar cladding, insulated glazing and concrete.

This three-storey house is located in a conservation area of De Beauvoir town in Hackney. The site has been excavated to basement level creating a sunken patio on which the house, a partly prefabricated solid timber structure, is placed. One enters the house at street level via parts of the lower ground floor roof, which also provide off street car parking. All façades of the house as well as the vertical and horizontal surfaces of the concrete patio are clad in timber rainscreen creating the impression of a continuous surface that embraces the enclosed and open spaces. The loadbearing structure of the house consists of large section engineered timber panels which have been manufactured off-site thereby limiting the on-site construction programme to approximately one week.

Das dreistöckige Haus liegt in dem Umwandlungsgebiet De Beauvoir town in Hackney. Es wurde zur Schaffung eines eingesunkenen Patios als teilweise vorgefertigte massive Holzkonstruktion in einer tiefen Baugrube errichtet. Man betritt das Haus an der Strassenseite auf einem Teil der Erdgeschossdecke, die auch einen Parkplatz bietet. Alle Fassaden des Hauses sowie die vertikalen und horizontalen Flächen des Betonpatios sind mit einer vorgehängten Fassade aus Holz verkleidet, so dass der Eindruck einer durchgehenden, sämtliche geschlossenen und offenen Räume umfassenden Oberfläche entsteht. Die tragende Struktur des Hauses besteht großteils aus bearbeiteten und vorgefertigten Holzpaneelen, so dass sich die Bauzeit vor Ort auf etwa eine Woche verkürzte.

← View to kitchen. Blick zur Küche.

↖ Dining room. Esszimmer.
↑ Exterior bird's eye view. Vogelperspektive.
← Living room featuring the Eames Lounge chair. Wohnzimmer mit Charles und Ray Eames Lounge Stuhl.
↗ View into kitchen and dining area from terrace. Blick von der Terrasse zu Küche und Essbereich.
↘ Floor plan. Grundriss.
↘↘ Detail of window and lightwell. Details von Fenster und Lichthof.

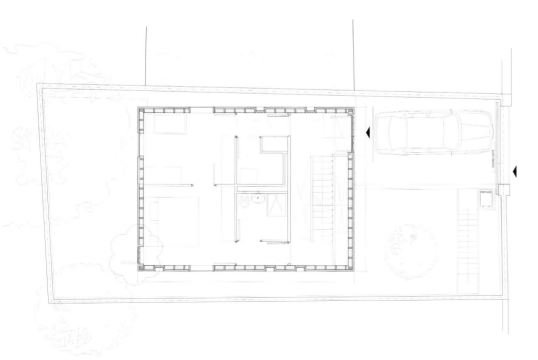

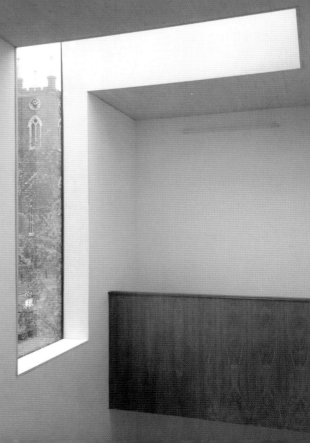

Typical of British interior design is...

maximising space and light with the use of new textures, finishes and colours.

Hampstead House

Blacksheep

Address: Bancroft Avenue, London N2. **Completion:** 2007. **Main function:** Living. **Materials:** Glass and wood.

The house purchased by Blacksheep's clients was a 1930s, two-storey, semi-detached house that had stood untouched for 30 years. The brief was to remodel the house on a strict budget, making it into a family home that fitted all their needs. Blacksheep created a completely new interior space plan, knocking out existing walls and looking to maximise the space. The plans, which received straightforward planning permission, included the creation of two roof dormers, transforming the loft into new and useful living space, the conversion of the ground floor garage into a dining area, and, on Blacksheep's suggestion, a glass-box extension to the rear of the house to extend the kitchen/diner area, with new exterior decking allowing the house to spill out into the rear garden space. As well as maximising space and light throughout the house, the new designs play on textures and finishes with colours and materials both linking and contrasting throughout.

Das Haus, das die Auftraggeber Blacksheeps gekauft hatten, war in den 1930er Jahren als zweigeschossige Doppelhaushälfte entstanden und seit 30 Jahren nicht verändert worden. Die Aufgabe bestand darin, den Bestand mit geringem Budget für die Bedürfnisse der Familie umzugestalten. Blacksheep veränderte den Innenausbau völlig, indem Wände ausgebrochen wurden und so größere Räume entstanden. Die Pläne, welche unkompliziert eine Baugenehmigung bekamen, umfassten das Einziehen zweier Dachgauben, die Umwandlung des Dachbodens in neue und nützliche Wohnfläche, die Umnutzung der Garage im Erdgeschoss in einen Essbereich, und – auf Vorschlag von Blacksheep – die rückwärtige Erweiterung des Hauses durch eine Glas-Box, die die Fläche von Küche und Esszimmer vergrößert und darüber hinaus mit der neuen Holzdeckung der Terrasse den Lebensraum in den Garten hinaus verlängert. Abgesehen von der Maximierung von Raum und Licht im ganzen Haus führt die Umgestaltung das Spiel mit verbindenden und kontrastierenden Texturen und Oberflächen in Farben und Materialien fort.

← View through kitchen. Blick durch die Küche.

↖ Master bedroom. Schlafzimmer der Eltern.
↑ Dining room. Esszimmer.
← Interior of new extension. Interieur der neuen Erweiterung.
↗ New rear glass-box extension. Rückwärtiger gläserner Anbau.
↘ Floor plan. Grundriss.
↘↘ Lounge. Lounge.

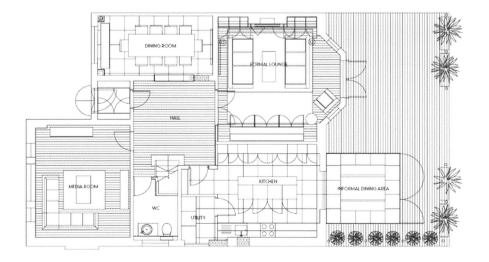

Floor plan labels: DINING ROOM, FORMAL LOUNGE, HALL, MEDIA ROOM, WC, UTILITY, KITCHEN, INFORMAL DINING AREA

Typical of British interior design is...

the use of reclaimed materials to create contemporary interiors that bring together the best of the historic and the now.

Black Lamb House

Paula Barnes

Address: Southease, Lewes, East Sussex BN7. **Client:** Paula Barnes and Matthew Thompson. **Completion:** 2009. **Main function:** Living. **Materials:** Rustic period fireplaces and reclaimed oak flooring.

Black Lamb House is a Grade II listed house in an ancient Sussex village next to a Norman church. The first half of the house was built in the 17th century with a later addition in the 18th. This 2009 extension uses many of the old elements of the house to inspire the new ones. 200 year old oak beams were sourced, ancient sinks brought in from Europe and doors with original glazing were found. Fireplaces were salvaged from both the UK and France. Newly lime rendered walls and beamed ceilings sit happily with the latest underfloor heating and insulation. Most of the interior furnishings consist of antiques or salvaged items, even down to the use of vintage fabrics for the curtains. Ironmongery, tiles and even the French doors were all reclaimed from other buildings. The unpainted, lime rendered walls and stone fireplaces gave the interior a well-worn feel from the moment it was finished. The result is a modern functional home set amongst the history of an ancient building.

Black Lamb House ist ein denkmalgeschütztes Haus neben einer normannischen Kirche in einem alten Dorf in Sussex. Der ältere Teil des Hauses wurde im 17. Jahrhundert erbaut und im 18. Jahrhundert erweitert. Die aktuelle Erweiterung nutzt zahlreiche der alten Elemente als Inspirationsquelle für Neues. 200 Jahre alte Eichenbalken wurden beschafft, alte Waschbecken vom europäischen Festland importiert und Türen mit Originalverglasung gesucht. Alte Kamine sowohl aus dem Vereinigten Königreich als auch aus Frankreich wurden hierher versetzt. Frisch gekalkte Wände und Balkendecken treffen nun mit modernster Fußbodenheizung und Wärmedämmung zusammen. Der Großteil der Innenausstattung besteht aus Antiquitäten oder Relikten, selbst die Stoffe der Vorhänge sind alt. Eisenwaren, Fliesen und sogar die französischen Türen wurden in anderen Bauten geborgt. Unbemalte mit Kalk verputzte Wände und die Steinkamine geben dem Interieur seit der Fertigstellung den Charme des sorgsam Benutzten. Das Ergebnis ist ein modernes, funktionales Zuhause vor der dem Hintergrund der Geschichte eines alten Gebäudes.

← Bedroom. Schlafzimmer.

↖ Living room featuring a vintage sofa. Wohnzimmer und historisches Sofa.

↑ Antique bathroom sink. Antikes Waschbecken.

← Living room with fireplace. Wohnzimmer mit Kamin.

↗ Interior. Interieur.

↘ Floor plans. Grundrisse.

↘↘ Kitchen. Küche.

shopping

a sense of utopian optimism, the belief that only dynamic, poetic design can come from innovative attempts to achieve the impossible.

Emperor Moth

Ab Rogers Design

Address: 93 Mount Street, Mayfair, London W1K 2SY. **Client:** Katia Gomiashvili. **Architectural Consultant:** DA.studio. **Graphic Design Consultant:** Praline. **Furniture:** Van Rooij & Griffiths. **Movement:** Asmech. **Interactive Consultant:** Robson & Jones. **Completion:** 2006. **Main function:** Shop. **Materials:** Polyurethane resin, tiles (floor), polycarbonate mirrors (walls and ceilings).

Katia Gomiashvili commissioned Ab Rogers Design to create a new store in Mayfair for her Moscow-based fashion label. Clothing itself comes alive when we wear it, moving with us as we walk, run, or dance. How can we bring it back to life when it hangs on the rack in the shop? The designers began with the idea that a still image can seem to be in motion when it is fractured, repeated and extended on all sides. They created a multi-faceted mirrored tent to occupy the space. Any object placed on display – and any visitor – can suddenly be seen from a variety of angles simultaneously. The studio created a series of animals – a crocodile, a peacock and a wild boar – to keep the clothing company in the mirrored tent. A series of life-size puppets wearing the Emperor Moth clothing dance throughout the shop, animated by motors and pulleys. Entering this space is a kind of transformation. Even a slight movement suddenly takes on an air of drama and dynamism. Each splash of colour becomes a new mosaic. Each light becomes a new constellation.

Katia Gomiashvili beauftragte Ab Rogers Design eine neue Boutique in Mayfair für ihr Moskauer Modelabel zu gestalten. Da Kleidung erst lebt, wenn sie von Menschen getragen wird, die sich beim Laufen, Rennen oder Tanzen bewegen, stellte sich die Frage, wie man sie im Geschäft an einem Kleiderständer zum Leben erwecken könne? Die Designer gingen davon aus, dass ein unbewegtes Bild bewegt erscheint, sobald es fragmentiert, wiederholt und allseitig erfasst werden kann. So schufen sie für den Raum ein Zelt mit facettierter Spiegeloberfläche. Jedes ausgestellte Objekt, aber auch jeder Besucher, ist hier sofort aus einer Vielzahl von Perspektiven erfassbar. Das Studio schuf Tierfiguren, welche die Modefirma in dem verspiegelten Zelt hütet – ein Krokodil, einen Pfau und ein Wildschwein. Eine Gruppe lebensgroßer Puppen, die Emperor Moth-Kleidung trägt, tanzt, von Motoren und Riemenscheiben angetrieben, durch das Geschäft. Wer den Raum betritt durchlebt eine Transformation – selbst kleine Bewegungen werden zu dramatischen und dynamischen Ereignissen, jeder Farbklecks wird zum Mosaik und jedes Licht zu einem neuen Sternbild.

← Polycarbonate mirror covering walls and ceiling. Polycarbonatspiegel überziehen Wände und Decke.

↖ Life-size puppets as hangers on racks. Lebensgroße Puppen als Kleiderbügel am Kleiderständer.
↑ View to multi-faceted mirrored tent. Ansicht des facettiert verspiegelten Zeltes.
← Wild boar on shop floor. Wildschwein auf dem Boden.
↗ Clothing displays seen from a variety of angles simultaneously. Kleiderpuppe, aus zahlreichen Winkeln gleichzeitig gesehen.
↘ Concept sketch. Ideenskizze.
↘↘ Detail of puppet hanger. Detail einer Kleiderbügelpuppe.

Typical of British interior design is...

melding instinctive, material sense
with a concern for timelessness.

Shop&Show

Karl Humphreys

Address: 1-5 Exhibition Road, Brompton, London SW7 2HE. **Client:** Tracey Neuls Footwear. **Artist and shoe designer:** Tracey Neuls. **Salvage / design:** Retrouvius. **Completion:** 2009. **Main function:** Shop. **Materials:** Salvaged wooden drawers and clamps, used as walls and show stands.

Coinciding with London Fashion Week 2009, Tracey Neuls created a temporary "shop and show" in Kensington. Her collection of shoe designs past, present and future, were showcased and sold for a period of three weeks. The shoes were hung from vertiginous towers made from hundreds of reclaimed vintage drawer units. The drawers were also arranged vertically and clamped together to form shelving. Amongst the shoes lurked an array of objects, muses and everyday, overlooked paraphernalia which inspires much of Tracey's work. Like Eileen Gray last century (to whom she has been compared) she is a designer who consistently shuns mainstream preoccupations with fashion, instead melding her instinctive, material sense with a concern for timelessness. Shop&Show offered a rare glimpse into her creative process.

Zeitgleich mit der London Fashion Week 2009, entstand das Interieur als temporäres „Shop and Show" für Tracey Neuls in Kensington. Vergangene, aktuelle und die nächste ihrer Kollektionen wurden für einen Zeitraum von drei Wochen präsentiert und verkauft. Die Schuhe hingen über Schwindel erregenden Türmen aus Hunderten gebrauchter, aufgearbeiteter Schubladen. Schubladen wurden auch vertikal getapelt und verklammert, um Regale zu bilden. Zwischen den Schuhen verstecken sich hintersinnige und alltägliche Objekte, unbeachterer Krimskrams, der Tracey Neuls Arbeit häufig inspiriert. Wie Eileen Gray im letzten Jahrhundert, mit der sie oft verglichen wird, meidet sie in ihrer Mode konsequent den Mainstream und versucht, ihre instinktiven Sinn für Material mit Zeitlosigkeit zu verschmelzen. Shop&Show bot einen seltenen Einblick, in den für sie typischen kreativen Prozess.

← Vintage drawer units as wall displays. Alte Schubladen als Wandschaukästen.

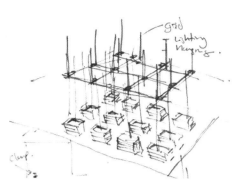

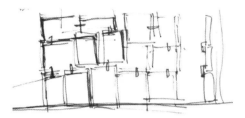

← ← Shoes hung over reclaimed vintage drawer units. Schuhe über neu genutzten alten Schubladen hängend.
← Vintage drawers stacked on top of each other. Alte, gestapelte Schubladen.
↑ Sketches. Skizzen.
↙ Interior with shoes hanging from ceiling. Interieur mit von der Decke hängenden Schuhen.
↓ Shoe display of drawers arranged vertically and clamped together to create shelving. Vertikale, gestapelte Schubladen, zu Regalen verklammert.

Typical of British interior design is...

being reminiscent of a fun place, rather than
a corporate entertainment space.

Kvadrat HQ

Adjaye Associates

Address: 10 Shepherdess Walk, London N1 7LB. **Client:** Kvadrat. **Graphic Designer:** Peter Saville. **Completion:** 2009. **Main function:** Office and showroom. **Materials:** Black resin floor, Dinesen Douglas Fir timber floor, black stained brickwork (original), lacquered MDF furniture and Flos lighting.

The new UK headquarters and showroom for Danish textiles company Kvadrat was designed by Adjaye Associates in collaboration with Peter Saville in the former premises of a Victorian factory. The showroom is a light-filled, double height, lower ground space with an office on a mezzanine floor. Part of the floor was removed to create a dramatic, singular hall-like space with a spectrum-coloured glass balustrade following the length of the staircase. The space will be used for events and a place to showcase art, design, and moving image creative endeavours which Kvadrat actively supports. It was also essential that Kvadrat was able to display the artist/designer special projects that it commissions. The feel of the space, however, is more reminiscent of a nightclub than a corporate entertainment space. The rustic wooden staircase at the entrance leads down to a basement dominated by muted greys and blacks. Textiles are on display here in cabinets that disappear into the wall leaving space for social events.

Der neue Hauptsitz mit Showroom der dänischen Textilfirma Kvadrat in London wurde von Adjaye Associates in Zusammenarbeit mit Peter Saville in einer ehemaligen viktorianischen Fabrik errichtet. Der Ausstellungsraum ist Licht durchflutet, zwei Geschosse hoch und bietet einem Büro Raum auf einem Zwischengeschoss. Ein Teil des Bodens wurde entfernt, um einen dramatischen, durchgehenden, hallenartigen Raum zu schaffen. Die Wangen der Treppe sind auf ganzer Länge mit Glas in Spektralfarben versehen. Der Raum wird für verschiedene Veranstaltungen und als Ausstellungsort für Kunst und Design insbesondere aber dem Film genutzt, dessen kreativen Ausdruck Kvadrat aktiv unterstützt. Es ist ein passender Rahmen, in dem Kvadrat den Künstlern und Designern seine speziellen Produkte präsentieren kann. Die Atmosphäre blieb, sollte jedoch eher der eines Nachtclubs als der eines Unterhaltungszentrums einer Firma entsprechen. Die rustikale Holztreppe am Eingang führt in einen Keller hinab, der von gedämpften Grau- und Schwarztönen dominiert wird. Textilien werden in Schränken präsentiert, die bei gesellschaftlichen Veranstaltungen in den Wänden verschwinden.

← Spectrum-coloured glass balustrade following the length of the staircase. Spektralfarbene Glaswangen entlang des gesamten Treppenlaufs.

↖ Office at mezzanine floor. Büro im Zwischengeschoss.
↑ Detail of staircase. Detail der Treppe.
← Double height showroom. Ausstellungsraum mit doppelter Raumhöhe.
↗ Hall-like space with a spectrum-coloured glass balustrade along the staircase. Hallenartiger Raum mit Glaswange in den Farben des Spektrums in ganzer Länge der Treppe.
↘ Floor plan. Grundriss.
↘↘ Detail staircase. Detail Treppe.

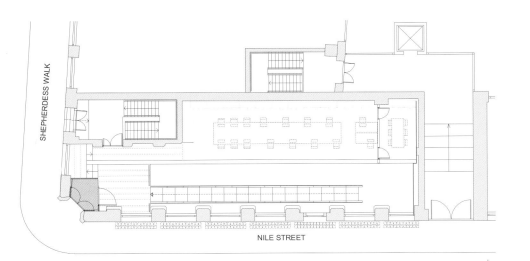

SHEPHERDESS WALK

NILE STREET

Typical of British interior design is...

the playful mixing of found bits of furniture from reclamation yards.

Tom Dixon Shop

Studio Toogood

Address: Portobello Dock, 344 Ladbroke Grove, London W10 5BU. **Client:** Tom Dixon. **Completion:** 2009. **Main function:** Shop. **Materials:** Concrete, stone, copper, cast iron and wood.

The new London Shop is part of Tom Dixon's new office complex in Portobello Dock, Ladbroke Grove. The interior showcases Faye Toogood's distinctive approach to design that disregards convention in favour of something altogether more brave, joyous and impulsive. Over 1800 square feet, the new Shop permanently displays the full Tom Dixon collection alongside Tom Dixon by George Smith upholstery pieces. The showroom is conceived as a stage set representing Tom Dixon's industrial aesthetic, with windows and walkways linking individual room sets within the warehouse. Visitors can explore the showroom by peering through these windows and doors into each room. The design is inspired by materials used in Dixon's designs, including copper, cast iron and wood.

Der neue Londoner Shop ist Teil der neuen Niederlassung Tom Dixons in Portobello Dock, Ladbroke Grove. Der Innenraum zeugt von Faye Toogoods unverwechselbarem Gestaltungsansatz, der Konventionen zugunsten einer mutigen, fröhlichen und impulsiven Gestaltung missachtet. Auf über 165 Quadratmetern präsentiert das Geschäft die vollständige Kollektion von Tom Dixon, inklusive der Tom Dixon Postermöbel von George Smith. Der Ausstellungsraum ist als Bühne für Tom Dixons industrielle Ästhetik konzipiert, und Fenster sowie Stege verbinden die einzelnen Szenerien innerhalb des Lagers. Besucher können in der Ausstellung durch Fenster und Türen in die einzelnen Räume spähen. Der Entwurf ist durch Materialien aus Dixons Designs, darunter Kupfer, Gusseisen und Holz, inspiriert.

← Individual wooden room display. Individueller hölzerner Ausstellungsraum.

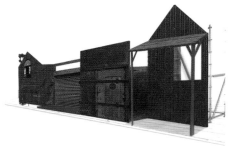

← ← Windows and walkways linking individual room sets within
the warehouse. Fenster und Stege verbinden Einzelraumszenarien im
Lagerhaus.

← 2009 Collection: Offcut and Slab stools. Kollektion der Offcut und Slab
stools von 2009.

↑ Axonometric. Axionometrie.

↙ Tom Dixon display collection and George Smith upholstery pieces. Tom
Dixon Auslage und George Smith Polstermöbel.

↓ Tom Dixon's product displays. Tom Dixons Produkte.

Typical of British interior design is...
the eclectic, honest and resourceful use of materials.

Regent Street Anthropologie

Anthropologie Store Design

Address: 158 Regent Street, London W1B 5SW. **Client:** Anthropologie. **Architect of record:** Tom Giannini Architects. **Completion:** 2009. **Main function:** Shop. **Materials:** Entry-Custom 'Parquet' concrete tile, white oak, polished concrete (floors), cast iron and glass treads (stair), artisan plaster perimeter and specialty plaster finish vignette panels (walls).

This design transformed an existing street level shop into a dynamic three-storey space, woven together with steel, vegetation and light. A light and open monumental stair and 200 square metre living wall respond to the natural light flooding into the store from the skylights over the site. The main steel staircase with cast iron and glass treads reinterprets the monumental stair and allows multiple paths of travel between levels from the front or back of the store. 14 different plant types inhabit the living wall, which stitches the three floors together and was conceived as a whimsical and more organic version of plaid fabric. The 'Parlour Room' at the front of the store has a custom concrete tile floor that is a modern interpretation of a traditional wood floor pattern. A steel clad threshold leads into the main sales floor which is dominated by reclaimed white oak, while the basement level walls are finished in plaster impressed with lace and the first floor dazzles in high-gloss white paint.

Der Entwurf verwandelt ein bestehendes Geschäft im Erdgeschoss in einen dynamischen, durch Stahl, Vegetation und Licht verwobenen, drei Stockwerke übergreifenden Raum. Eine große, helle und offene Treppe sowie eine 200 Quadratmeter große begrünte Wand bringen das durch die Oberlichter in den gesamten Laden flutende Tageslicht zur Geltung. Die Haupttreppe aus Stahlguss mit Glasstufen erfindet die Monumentaltreppe neu und gestattet verschiedene Wege zwischen den Ebenen der Vorder- und Rückseite des Geschäfts. Die begrünte Wand aus 14 verschiedenen Pflanzenarten verbindet die drei Etagen. Sie wurde als skurrile und ökologischere Variante eines Plaid-Stoffes angelegt. Der „Salon" im Eingangsbereich zeigt mit eigens entworfenen Betonfliesen eine moderne Interpretation eines traditionellen Holzparkett-Musters. Eine Stahl verkleidet Schwelle führt in den wichtigsten Verkaufsbereich, der von weißer Eichenverkleidung dominiert wird, während im Untergeschoss Wände aus Gips mit aufgedruckter Spitze den Raum prägen und die erste Etage in hochglänzender weißer Farbe erstrahlt.

← Fitting room entry. Eingang zur Umkleidekabine.

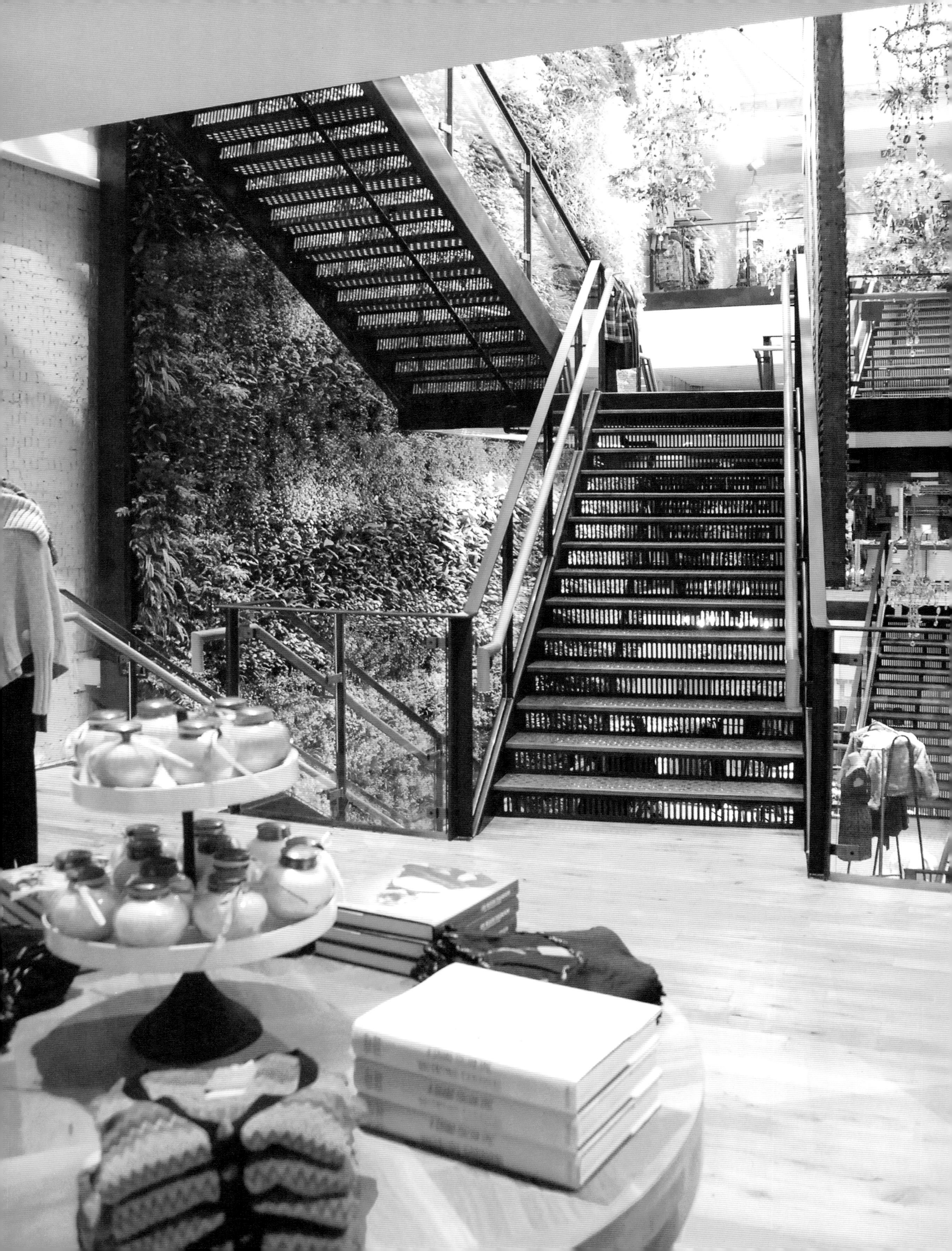

←← Monumental cast iron and glass treads stair and green wall.
Monumentale Gusseisentreppe mit Glasstufen und begrünter Wand.
← Basement floor sales area. Verkaufsraum im Keller.
↙ Entry parlour. Eingangssalon.
↓ First floor sales area at front of store. Verkaufsbereich im vorderen
Gebäudeteil des ersten Obergeschosses.

Typical of British interior design is...
raw simplicity of the
concept and materials.

Sneaker Department, Dover Street Market

Studio Toogood

Address: 17-18 Dover Street, London W1S 4LT. **Client:** Commes des Garçons. **Completion:** 2009. **Main function:** Shop. **Materials:** Plaster boxes, copper piping, concrete and rope.

London's legendary Dover Street Market has just revamped its basement by giving it a clean new look. As part of this transformation, Faye Toogood was asked to design and install a new sneaker department that could sit alongside Rai Kawakubo's personal vision. Faye wanted to create a raw but elegant space and chose to work with plaster, concrete, copper and rope. She was not aiming for a glossy, highly finished look but rather to reveal the nature of the materials themselves and their inherent imperfections, or inherent beauty. A series of stacking building blocks made from plaster were designed to help re-configure and change the way the space is used. The purity of the white plaster contrasts with the roughness of the rendered concrete walls and a series of interlocking copper pipes provide a strong industrial element to the design as well as providing plinths for the more practical purpose of displaying multi-coloured sneakers. The space is lit by bulbs on rope by Christien Meindertsma.

Das Kellergeschoss von Londons legendärem Dover Street Market erhielt ein reduziertes neues Erscheinungsbild. Faye Toogood wurde gebeten, eine neue Turnschuh-Abteilung zu gestalten, die mit dem individuellen Geschmack Rai Kawakubos einhergehen konnte. Faye wollte einen rustikalen, aber eleganten Raum schaffen und wählte Putz, Beton, Kupfer und Seil als Materialien. Ziel war, kein glänzendes, perfektes Erscheinungsbild zu schaffen, sondern die Eigenarten der Materialien selbst und die ihnen innewohnenden Unzulänglichkeiten, ihre ureigene Schönheit zu offenbaren. Gestapelte Gipsbausteine wurden entwickelt und gefertigt, um den Raum und seine Konfiguration neu zu definieren. Die Makellosigkeit des weißen Putzes kontrastiert mit den schroff verputzten Betonwänden. Eingearbeitete Kupferrohre betonen nicht nur das industrielle Element im Entwurf, sie dienen auch ganz praktisch dem Arrangement der mehrfarbigen Turnschuhe. Der Raum wird von Christien Meindertsmas Glühbirnen am Seil beleuchtet.

← Stacking building plaster blocks as wall and floor product displays.
Gestapelte Gipsbaustein als Wand- und Bodendisplays.

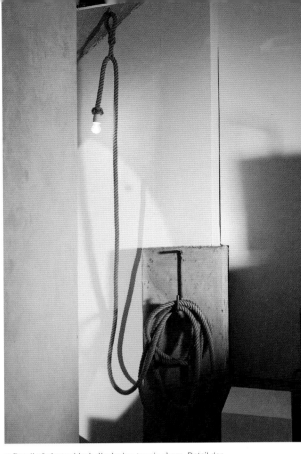

↖ Detail of plaster block displaying tennis shoes. Detail der Gipsbausteine, auf denen Tennisschuhe zur Schau destellt werden.
↑ Rope lighting system. Lichtseilsystem.
← General interior view. Totale des Innenraums.
↗ Interior perspective view. Innenraumpespektive.
↘ Sketch. Skizze.
↘↘ Detail of plaster boxes display. Detail des Gipsbausteinarrangements.

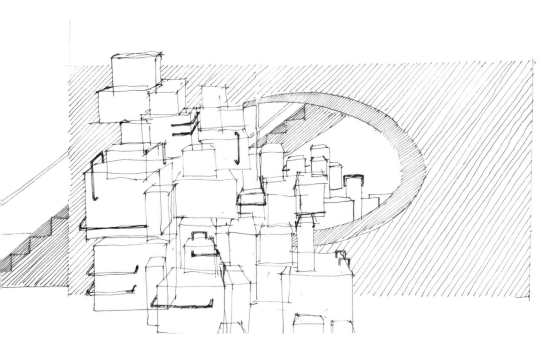

Typical of British interior design is...

the incorporation of the beautiful and miraculous principles of nature.

Camper Store

Tokujin Yoshioka

Address: 207-209 Regent Street, London W1B 4ND. **Client:** Camper. **Completion:** 2009. **Main function:** Shop. **Materials:** Artificial suede.

Plants, flowers and other elements found in the natural world can please us with their ever-changing appearance. The idea for this new store, which incorporates such beautiful and miraculous principles of nature, is derived from the installation presented in New York in 2007, where approximately 30,000 sheets of tissue paper were used to cover the entire space and create a scene reminiscent of a snowscape. On designing the new store concept for Camper, the leading Spanish shoe brand, Tokujin Yoshioka contemplated how to create a new style by embracing both Camper's brand identity and his own original design concepts, following on from Camper's previous collaborations with distinctive international creators. The red flower blossoms with an emphasis on the corporate colour are in full bloom in the store. It expresses the nature of the tissue installation on a more permanent basis.

Pflanzen, Blumen und andere Elemente der Natur erfreuen den Menschen in ihrer immer wechselnden Erscheinung. Die Idee, diese Filiale von Camper mit solch anmutenden und zauberhaften Prinzipien der Natur zu verwandeln, geht auf eine New Yorker Gestaltung von 2007 zurück, bei der ca. 30.000 Bögen Seidenpapier verwendet wurden, um den gesamten Raum einzukleiden und in eine, einer Schneelandschaft ähnelnden Szenerie zu verwandeln. Bei der Gestaltung des neuen Store Concepts für die führende spanische Schuhmarke Camper wollte Tokujin Yoshioka einen neuen Stil kreieren, der sowohl Campers Markenidentität als auch seine originellen Design-Konzepte vereint, und an die früheren Kooperationen Campers mit bekannten internationalen Designern anknüpft. Die roten Blüten, die die Hausfarbe Campers betonen, stehen in voller Blüte. Sie sind eine dauerhafter Hinweis auf die Art der Installation.

← Wall covered in folded artificial red suede. Wand mit gefaltetem Wildleder.

↖ Yoshioka's Bouquet chair for Moroso, made using folded tissue technique. Yoshioka's Bouquet chair für Moroso mit gefalteten Geweben.
↑ Detail wall with folded artificial red suede. Detail der Wand mit gefaltetem roten Kunstwildleder.
← Wall and chairs covered using the folded tissue technique. Wand und Stühle, an Schneelandschaft erinnernd.
↗ General interior view. Totale des Interieurs.
↘ Section. Schnitt.
↘↘ Detail of Moroso chairs. Detail des Moroso Stuhls.

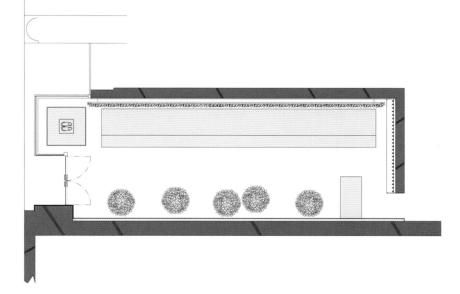

Typical of British interior design is...
the use of ornaments and colours to give a strong visual character to the interior.

Liverpool Paradise Pavilion

FAT

Address: Paradise Street, Liverpool, Merseyside L1. **Client:** Grosvenor. **Other creatives:** Waterman Structures and Hoare Lea Engineers. **Completion:** 2008. **Main function:** Restaurant and shops. **Materials:** Ceramic tile on steel frame structure.

FAT won a competition to design a two-storey building as part of the Paradise Street Development Area scheme in Liverpool city centre. The design introduces an intriguing and delightful new building into the Church Yard Arcade, using references that include ornamental and decorative street furniture as well as the tiled and patterned façades of the Victorian buildings of Liverpool. FAT's approach was to design a building within a building, distinct from its surroundings and acting as a gateway or landmark to the new development. The façade is expressed as a decorative tiled screen and the series of facets along it alter the building's interior spaces and provide niches for seating and views into Church Yard from the first floor café and ground floor retail units. Shop fronts are as large as possible and all windows are tall and vertical in aspect. The 'screen' diminishes at either end to lower points to create a comfortable junction between the arcade and the pavilion.

FAT gewann einen Wettbewerb zur Gestaltung eines zweistöckigen Gebäudes im Paradise Street Entwicklungsgebiet des Stadtzentrums von Liverpool. Der Entwurf ergänzt die Church Yard Passage um ein interessantes und reizvolles neues Gebäude, das sowohl Verbindungen zu ornamentalem und dekorativem Stadtmobiliar aufnimmt, als auch mit den gemusterten Fliesen und Fassaden Beziehungen zu viktorianischen Gebäuden Liverpools aufbaut. FAT gestaltete ein Gebäude in einem Gebäude, das sich von seiner Umgebung abhebt und als Tor oder Wahrzeichen des Entwicklungsgebiets dient. Die Fassade versteht sich als dekorative Fliesenfläche, während die Erkerreihe das Innere des Gebäudes verändert und den Sitzgelegenheiten im Café des Obergeschosses und den Verkaufsflächen im Erdgeschoss einen Blick auf den Church Yard beschert. Die Geschäftsfronten sind möglichst groß gestaltet und sämtliche Fenster sind hochformatig, einen vertikalen Aspekt ausbildend. Die Fassadenfläche senkt sich an beiden Enden herab um einen angenehmen Übergang zwischen den Arkaden und dem Pavillon zu ermöglichen.

← Detail of polychromatic tiles. Detail der vielfarbigen Fliesen.

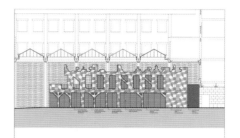

←← Glazed arcade housing a café and two shop units. Verglaste Passage mit einem Café und zwei Geschäften.

← Café. Café.

↑ Sections. Schnitte.

↙ Detail of polychromatic tiles and windows. Detail der vielfarbigen Fliesen und der Fenster.

↓ Wall with polychromatic tiles. Wand mit farbigen Fliesen.

Typical of British interior design is...

to celebrate the intrinsic character of the spaces and complement them with new and unexpected ones

King's Road Anthropologie

Anthropologie Store Design

Address: 131-141 King's Road, London SW3 4PW. **Completion:** 2010. **Main function:** Shop. **Materials:** Concrete encaustic floor tile, white oak, fumed finish floors, custom 'wood-cast' concrete tiles, polished concrete floor, Artisan plaster perimeter and specialty plaster finish vignette panels.

Originally the site of a billiard hall and garage, Anthropologie stripped the buildings back to structure and reinstated all of the decorative glass details, wood storefront, and skylights. Passing through the main entrance highlighted by colourful encaustic concrete tile and chandeliers, the visitor arrives in the former billiard hall. This space with its high vaulted ceilings and decorative steel trusses has been finished with a reclaimed maple parquet floor. In the centre of the space is a steel vignette, comprised of recombined components of a vintage French shop front. A large cascading stairway flowing through a portal of reclaimed barn wood forms a gentle transition between the billiard hall and garage. The garage floor is polished concrete to reflect the nature of the former space, while beautiful sawtooth skylights flood the space with natural light. The industrial feel is balanced by the colourful and eclectic artisan plaster vignette walls that surround the space.

Die ehemalige Billard-Halle und Garage wurde von Anthropologie bis auf den Kern rückgebaut und anschließend wieder mit dem dekorativen Glas, der hölzernen Geschäftsfassade und den Oberlichtern versehen. Das Gebäude wird durch den Haupteingang mit eindrucksvoller Betonplatten-Enkaustik und Kronleuchtern betreten. Dieser Raum mit hoher, gewölbter Decke und dekorativen Stahlträgern erhielt ein aufgearbeitetes Ahornparkett. In der Raummitte befindet sich eine Stahlgruppe, die aus neu angeordneten Komponenten einer alten französischen Ladenfront besteht. Eine große Treppe stuft sich durch ein Portal aus aufgearbeitetem Scheunenholz sanft von der ehemalige Billard-Halle zur umgestalteten Garage herab. Der Garagen-boden besteht, die ehemalige Funktion des Raums reflektierend, aus poliertem Beton, während durch schöne Sägezahn-Dachfenster natürliches Licht in den Raum flutet. Das industrielle Ambiente bildet ein Gleichgewicht mit dem vielfältigen und farbigen Gipsputz der Mauern des Raums.

← Entry hall. Eingangshalle.

↖ Stair platform display. Ausstellung auf Treppenabsatz.
↑ View into former 'Garage' space. Blick in die ehemalige Garage.
← Fitting rooms. Umkleidekabine.
↗ Anthropologie gallery space. Anthropologie Galerieraum.
↘ Floor plan. Grundriss.
↘↘ Dining vignette. Essgruppe.

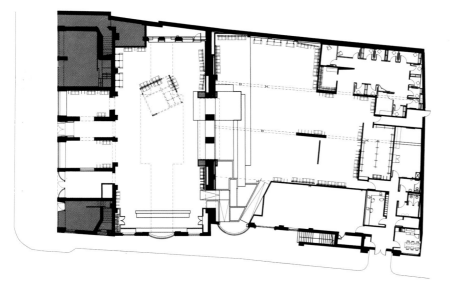

Index